Thames & Hudson

THE NILE

From the Mountains
to the Mediterranean

Aldo Pavan

with 207 illustrations, 183 in colour

CONTENTS

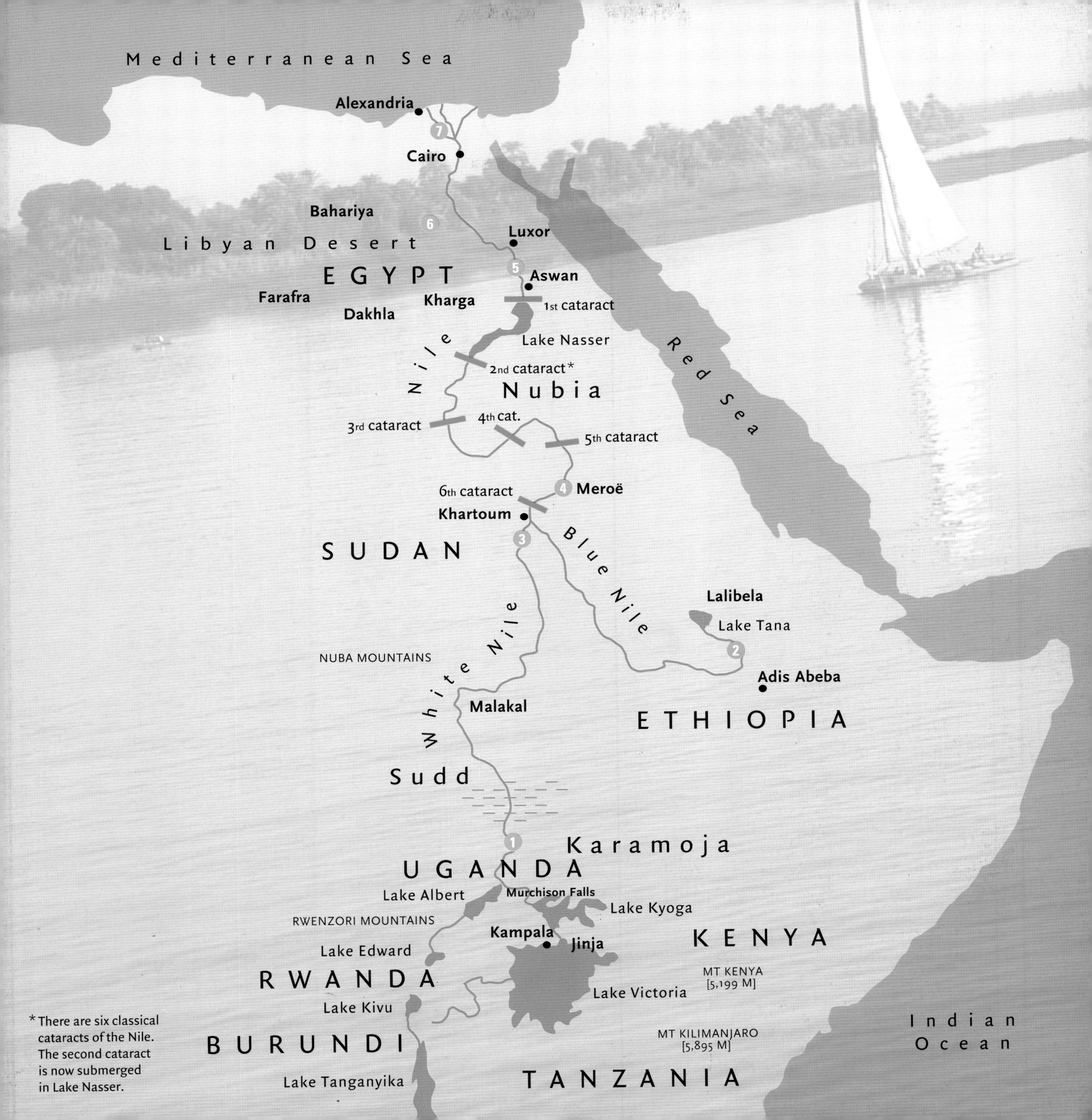

Mediterranean Sea

Alexandria
7
Cairo

Bahariya
6
EGYPT
Luxor
5
Aswan
Farafra
Kharga
1st cataract
Dakhla
Lake Nasser

Libyan Desert

Nile
2nd cataract *
Nubia
3rd cataract
4th cat.
5th cataract

6th cataract
4
Meroë
Khartoum
3

SUDAN

Blue Nile

Red Sea

Lalibela
Lake Tana

White Nile

NUBA MOUNTAINS

Adis Abeba

Malakal

ETHIOPIA
2

Sudd

1

Karamoja

UGANDA

Lake Albert
Murchison Falls
Lake Kyoga

RWENZORI MOUNTAINS

KENYA

Lake Edward
Kampala
Jinja

RWANDA

MT KENYA
[5,199 M]

Lake Kivu
Lake Victoria

* There are six classical
cataracts of the Nile.
The second cataract
is now submerged
in Lake Nasser.

BURUNDI

MT KILIMANJARO
[5,895 M]

Indian
Ocean

Lake Tanganyika

TANZANIA

The waterfall of Tis Isat on the Blue Nile, Ethiopia. Lake Tana, 30 kilometres upriver, is considered to be the source of this section of the river.

OPPOSITE: (left) In Uganda the line of the Equator is marked by a circular structure; (right) Small painted grain stores in the Nubian Desert in Sudan.

OVERLEAF: (page 16, left) The Nile laps the temples on the island of Philae, near Aswan; (page 16, right, and page 17) The columns of the temple of Karnak at Luxor, and a bas-relief from Luxor Temple, showing two images of Hapy, god of the Nile and symbol of fertility.

THE NILE IS STEEPED IN THE ROOTS OF HISTORY.

THE NILE IS STEEPED IN THE ROOTS OF HISTORY. It is part of the genetic make-up of Western culture. It conjures up images of pyramids and pharaohs, temples and tombs, underground chambers in which gold and jewels lie hidden, mummies, sarcophagi and hieroglyphics; silt, which has fertilized the ground for thousands of years of civilization; and water, a long strip of blue traversing the desert, an oasis stretching for hundreds of miles. For centuries it has been a granary, providing rice, cotton, wheat and lush green palm trees. It has been venerated in the form of a god named Hapy, and has been considered to be the very centre of the world. Indeed, Egypt and the pharaonic civilization owe their existence to the river.

The Nile is more than that, however. It has not only nourished the soul of Egypt, but of seven further nations: Burundi, Rwanda, Tanzania, Kenya, Uganda, Ethiopia and Sudan. Its drainage basin extends over three million square kilometres – 3,349,000 square kilometres to be precise. The destiny of this river is intertwined with that of hundreds of millions of people – a world in which people with characteristic proud features epitomize Africa, an area of breathtaking beauty and the cradle of humanity. Though well known for its role in the history of Egypt, the Nile also has thousands of unknown faces: obscure or rarely observed events that are far removed from the world stage. Births, deaths, love, war, famine and hope – all have occurred here, across the sweep of the Great Lakes and the western part of the Rift Valley.

Flowing roughly 6,695 kilometres from its source to its mouth, the Nile is the longest river in the world and penetrates the very heart of Africa. From Burundi, the first gushes of water trickle through Rwanda and Tanzania, until they finally transform themselves into the full force of a river in Uganda, where the Nile separates off from the huge Lake Victoria. Here nature is overwhelming, with lions, elephants and giraffe. Waterfalls and rapids pour out a shimmering blue into the yellow savannah. At times, it encounters swathes of impenetrable jungle, home to gorillas.

Having swept up the tragedy of the endless guerrilla war in the north of Uganda, the Nile then loses itself in the swamps of Sudan, in the southern region whose name in Arabic means 'obstacle'. It forks into many branches bearing exotic names, such as Gazelle River, Giraffe River and Mountain River, but the reality

is much less poetic, for this part of Africa tragically remains under the tyranny of the Kalashnikov. Peace was only achieved in 2005, after twenty years of fighting between Muslims and Christians, Arabs and non-Arabs.

At Khartoum, the capital of Sudan, the waters of the White Nile converge with the waters of the Blue Nile, which flow down from the Ethiopian Plateau and Lake Tana. Coursing through the desert, before entering Egypt, the river traverses the Nubian Desert, the historic region of ancient pharaohs, rich in archaeological treasures. From here on, the river takes on its familiar face: Lake Nasser and Abu Simbel, the Ptolemaic temples, Aswan and Luxor. It is the Nile in all its splendour, in all its magnificence.

Along its banks are the visible traces of the earliest spread of Christianity, with churches and Coptic monasteries. In the Egyptian desert, the Gospel had evolved into a form of mystic self-discipline, before the sword of Islam held sway in the sixth century. The most ancient heart of Cairo is the Christian district, which was once based on the banks of the Nile. Today, Coptic Cairo is a precious relic.

Escaping the many tentacles of the modern capital, the Nile hurries towards the Mediterranean, where it flows into an immense delta. The city of Alexandria rises up on its western banks. Here, the heart of Africa dissolves into classical culture, and into the deep roots of the European soul. It is a metaphorical synthesis, of which only the Nile could be the architect.

CHAPTER ONE

Uganda: The Infinite Source of the Nile

AT JINJA, THE SLUGGISH WATERS OF LAKE VICTORIA pick up speed around a sharp bend on the northern edge; they seem to become more animated, tumbling over rocks and increasing in momentum, rippling into ever more impetuous rapids. The fishermen's boats are tossed about like small twigs. A stone proclaims to the visitor with indisputable certainty that this is the beginning of the Nile: 'This spot marks the place from where the Nile starts its long journey to the Mediterranean Sea through central and northern Uganda, Sudan and Egypt.' An unequivocal statement, or so it would seem. However, quite some distance away another sign makes more or less the same claim, with the same degree of authority.

Caput Nili is written on a metal plaque attached to a stone pyramid at the source of the river Kagera, the biggest tributary of Lake Victoria at 690 kilometres long. According to some geographers, these waters which flow from Burundi, through Rwanda and Tanzania into Uganda, and then into Lake Victoria itself, may well be the true and most distant source of the Nile. In 1937 a German explorer named Burkhart Waldecker uncovered this possibility when he reached the source of the Kagera River and saw a rivulet gushing out of fertile terrain. He christened this stream the Nile.

How vanity can cloud judgment! Closer inspection would have revealed that the Nile actually begins even further south. In fact the Kagera itself is fed by the river Luvironza, which begins in the southern plateaus of Burundi, 45 kilometres east of Lake Tanganyika. From here, the river creates the river Ruvubu and only then, after 350 kilometres, does it flow into the Kagera itself.

The impossibility of establishing the true source of the longest river on the planet has proved to be a hydrographical enigma. During the nineteenth century, this riddle caused scores of English explorers to put their lives in danger, in the hope of setting eyes on the first spurt of the river of the pharaohs, and then being able to regale the salons of the Royal Geographical Society with their tales.

The Kagera is just one of many tributaries that flow into Lake Victoria from the surrounding mountains. The lake acts as an impluvium, collecting and draining the waters of a vast area into an enormous basin. Perhaps, as Ptolemy thought in the second century AD, it really was the Mountains of the Moon that gave birth to the river. If this is the case, the true origins of the river would have been the glaciers of Rwenzori, 'the rain-maker', at an altitude of over 5,000 metres. Or perhaps not; it is hard to say. The Nile, born of so many different rivers, is such a magnificent geographical mystery that each person can choose his own preferred source.

We are now back at the turbulent waters of Jinja. This is Uganda, a bewitching and magical country inhabited by the Baganda people. They have finally been left in peace following years of dictatorship under Idi Amin (1971–79), who was responsible for the deaths of some 300,000 opponents, and guerrilla war and human rights abuses under Milton Obote (1980–85), which resulted in a further 100,000 deaths.

At this point the Nile is known as the Victoria Nile. It was here that British explorer John Hanning Speke (1827–64), a former officer of the Indian army, arrived in 1858 after a very long voyage. He believed he had discovered the 'true' source of the Nile at Lake Victoria, but he had only discovered a part of the truth. The mystery of the source was to remain a riddle for many decades to come.

Jinja is a concentration of colonial villas, which are slightly crumbling, decorated in warm colours, and immersed in the all-consuming humidity. With its porches painted in pastel shades, it is the most beautiful city in Uganda. At the lakeside port, the fishermen are emptying their nets of *tilapia*, a fish that is sold in at least half the markets of Europe. Slightly further away from the centre, the boats depart for the islands on Lake Victoria. There are no quays: the boatmen carry the passengers on their shoulders to reach their boats beyond the sandbanks. As well as brightly dressed men and women, the boats are loaded up with bunches of green bananas, bicycles, crates of beer and sacks of coal.

Everyday life on this continent.... A young boy plunges his bicycle into the water, turns it upside down, and starts to clean it. A woman waits while her husband performs a similar operation on a machine half-immersed in water, with just sufficient depth before the lake disappears into the mud. Farther off, the landscape of the lake is animated by a sudden movement: fishermen are throwing their net into the air, and in mid-flight it is transformed into a giant butterfly, before falling into the water and ensnaring a shoal of fish. Suddenly birds are hovering in the hope of catching a fish that has escaped.

You could spend hours watching African life unfold before your eyes. The Nile seems to be aware of the fascination it creates, and snakes conceitedly away towards the valley. Almost at once it comes up against the first big dam constructed by man to impede its progress. Then it gathers momentum again and is seized by rapids. Eight kilometres further on, it reaches the tumultuous cascades at Bujagali, where it can display its full strength.

In the fierce afternoon heat, a fisherman from the tiny village of Kahendero takes a siesta on the banks of Lake George, in the Queen Elizabeth National Park.

OVERLEAF: Just before sunset, a herd of buffalo come down to quench their thirst and cool down in the waters of the Kazinga Channel, which links the vast Lake Edward and Lake George.

THESE PAGES AND OVERLEAF: Fishing on Lake George. Both men and women are involved in this work. The most sought-after species of fish is the Nile perch (*Lates Albertianus*), which is known as *capitain* in African French. The weight of the fish varies between 20 and 40 kilograms. Originally from the northern waters of the Nile, the fish has been introduced into many lakes in Uganda. Another common fish, particularly in Lake Victoria, is the *tilapia* (*Tilapia Nilotica*). At the end of the morning's work in Hamukungu, the catches of fish are weighed by the merchants and loaded into pick-up trucks, which then depart for the small towns dotted on the dusty slopes of the savannah.

Daily life on Lake Victoria, the largest of the African lakes, with shores bordering Uganda, Tanzania and Kenya. It has a surface area of almost 70,000 square kilometres and lies 1,134 metres above sea level. The Kagera River, its tributary, is considered to be one of the main sources of the Nile. Its banks are covered with dense vegetation and a rich variety of wildlife. The lake has only one distributary, the Nile, which at that point is called Victoria.

LEFT: The legs of a salt collector are smeared with pitch to protect his skin from scalding during long periods of immersion in the alkaline waters of the crater of the Katwe volcano.

RIGHT: The Queen Elizabeth National Park is characterized by a series of extinct volcanic craters. The bases of some of these craters are used for the extraction of salt. This activity was documented in the twelfth century and since then little, if anything, has changed in the production of this precious element. Not far from the banks of Lake George, the saltpans have a woven texture.

OVERLEAF: A sailing boat on Lake Victoria, with storm clouds gathering overhead.

Silverback is a contrary character. He emits guttural noises, which do not sound particularly friendly. The park ranger replies, using the same language. Man and gorilla, face to face. We are two metres away from this male, a mountain gorilla with black fur, weighing around two and a half tons. Now Silverback curls up, and his family gathers around him. There are females, and young of different ages, who have just finished stuffing their mouths with giant ants. They are settling down for a nap. It took us three hours to get here, deep in the heart of the Bwindi Forest. We are side by side with this family, which seems so reminiscent of our human family, all cuddled up together. The females stroke their babies. One is suckling. Then they pick fleas off each other. The male nods off, closes his eyes, and starts to snore.... Two babies scamper up a creeper and start jumping around up in the branches. Suddenly something falls down onto Silverback and he wakes with a start, leaps to his feet, seizes a large branch above his head, and tears at it with an almighty crash. It is cataclysmic. We tremble....

LEFT: A lioness sleeping on the branch of a tree during the hottest part of the day.

RIGHT: A glimpse of the Albert Nile, with a pair of Uganda kob antelope.

OVERLEAF: Some unexpected tea plantations seem to form a second skin over the undulating hills between Fort Portal and the Kibale Forest. As in colonial times, management of the plantations remains in the hands of foreign, mostly European companies. The government, which owns most of the land, is also encouraging small enterprises in order to stimulate growth in a sector that is close to collapse.

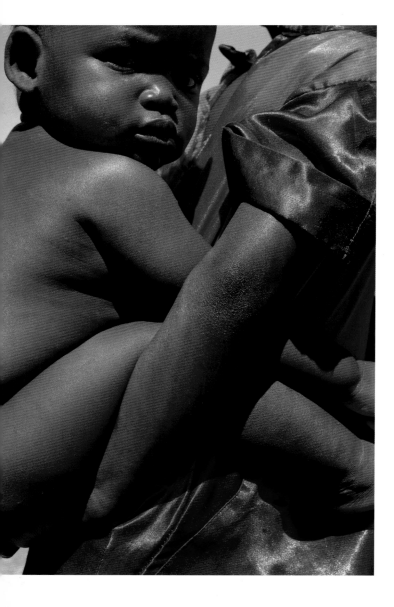

LEFT: In a village near Masindi, a small boy is carried on his sister's back.

RIGHT: Sunday in the small town of Hoima. These three women are all wearing the typical Ugandan costume.

OVERLEAF: A class in an elementary school in a small village on the Victoria Nile. Nobody wears shoes.

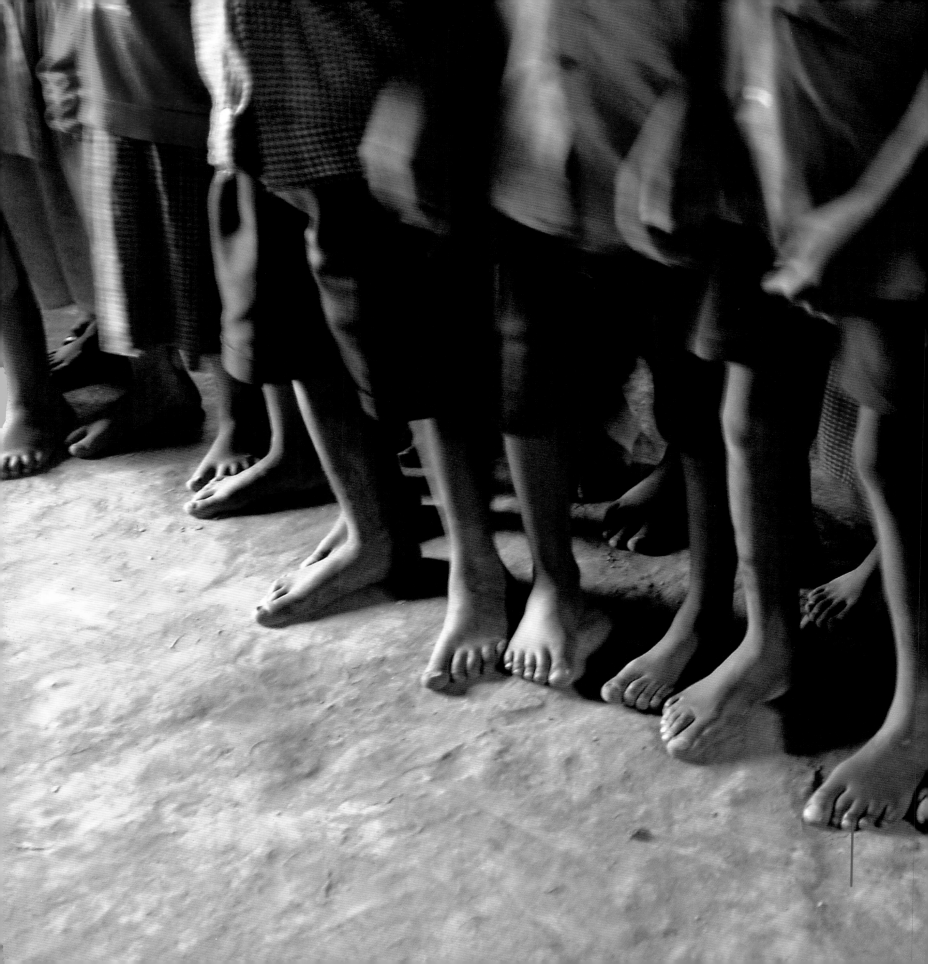

Jinja, at first light. Fishermen cast their nets over Lake Victoria. Most of them depend on fishing to earn their daily crust. The ecological equilibrium of the lake has been severely threatened by the construction of two hydroelectric dams. Since 2003, when the second power plant was opened, the water levels have sunk dramatically, which has had a major impact on the region.

Uganda on the one side, the Democratic Republic of Congo on the other. The ice peaks of the Rwenzori Mountains, which touch the skies, melt into water that flows as far as the Mediterranean – a journey of around 6,000 kilometres. Perhaps the white pinnacles in the heart of Africa are reflections of the pyramids of the pharaohs. The waters from the Rwenzori are one of many sources of the Nile. They descend into the valley in a thousand streams, filling up Lake Edward and Lake George, before the Semliki River collects up the waters and transports them into Lake Albert. This is another corner of Africa, beautiful and highly evocative: Hemingway's Africa. There are pockets of lost savannah, where crocodiles, hippopotamuses, giraffe, lions and elephants live in symbiosis with the great river. And birds, an infinite variety of birds. There is a sense of utter peace, harmony with nature, and beauty in abundance.

To think that only a few miles north the land is scarred by persecution and killings: the rebel brigades of the Lord's Resistance Army, an armed force that has been active since the 1980s, under the command of Joseph Kony, an Acholi, are fighting the Ugandan central government forces. Over the years thousands of children have been abducted and forced to enlist in the rebel ranks. The ultimate aim is reportedly to establish a regime based on the strict enforcement of the Ten Commandments.

As soon as the great river has left Lake Albert behind, it joins forces with its sister river, the Victoria Nile, which flows from Lake Victoria, culminating in the mighty and magnificent Murchison Falls. The river narrows and is forced through a gap in the rocks, dropping in three successive cascades of water, before it finds itself again 120 metres below, filling the air with a dusty dampness. In 1862 the English explorer Samuel Baker (1821–93) was dazzled by the sight of these falls and named them after the president of the Royal Geographical Society. Baker subsequently reached Lake Albert, thereby proving that there was no single source of the Nile.

This vast area of national park, the largest in Uganda, is named after the spectacular Murchison Falls. Here, the Nile is forced through a narrow gorge and thunders down a huge drop, throwing up foam, spray and clouds of mist into the surrounding jungle. Since 1961, when there were violent rainstorms and severe floods, the river has abandoned its original route and flows in two almost parallel courses.

OVERLEAF: Before going to school, two boys refill their water cans at a fountain.

LEFT: A woman carrying bunches of bananas emerges from the jungle along the Victoria Nile.

RIGHT: Jungle fires along the street that runs from Hoima to Lake Albert. In spring farmers start fires on purpose, in order to clear patches of land for cultivation. This makes the air stifling and at times almost obscures the sun. Part of the green heart of Uganda is being consumed by the flames as a result of this custom.

LEFT: The ferry from Paraa ploughs through the waters of the Victoria Nile, under the watchful gaze of a hippopotamus. From here, it is possible to travel by boat as far as the Murchison Falls. Along this stretch there is a succession of wildlife: crocodiles, elephants, antelope, warthogs and occasionally lions, easily visible to the naked eye. The hippopotamus is the king of these waters, however, retiring to the forest only after sunset. The great river also provides a habitat for an extraordinary variety of birdlife: African eagles, herons, spoonbills, ibis and cormorants all frequent its territory.

OPPOSITE: After the Murchison Falls, the Nile widens out beyond recognition and is covered in papyrus plants.

The small nine-seater Cessna belongs to a special aviation company, the Mission Aviation Fellowship, which connects the Ugandan capital Kampala with more remote mission fields. Pilots and mechanics are obliged to study the Bible before being allowed to fly with this company.

To the east, the earth becomes increasingly arid; the savannah has almost become a desert. This is Karamoja, home of the Karamojong people, a nomadic, warrior community of Nilotic-Hamitic origin, who arrived here from the northern savannah areas of modern Kenya. Their name derives from *aikar*, 'to stop', and *imojong*, 'ancient people'. Both feared and hated by neighbouring peoples such as the Turkana, the Pokot and the Teso, the Karamojong have a reputation for anarchy and plundering. Proud of their tradition, they are indomitable rebels and have been the bane of every public administration, from the English colonials who proclaimed their territory a prohibited area, to the independent government of Uganda. The men are armed, with Kalashnikovs slung over their shoulders. Their villages, which are enclosures surrounded by thorn bushes, are always in a state of war, with episodic violent clashes breaking out between the different clans, those from the plains or those from the hills.

As a result, Karamoja remains to this day semi-isolated from the rest of the country. Anyone who ventures into this territory puts his life at risk. That does not deter the Comboni Missionaries, or the doctors from the nearby hospital run by the humanitarian organization CUAAM, who live in Matany, a village on the Kenyan border. 'I don't think about death, otherwise I would live in fear,' explains Father Damian, who has come to terms with life in this belligerent corner of Africa.

The silhouette of a Karamojong shepherd at dawn, heading towards his herd of oxen. Karamoja, an extremely arid region in north-east Uganda, is unsafe for visitors owing to various conflicts involving military and rebel groups.

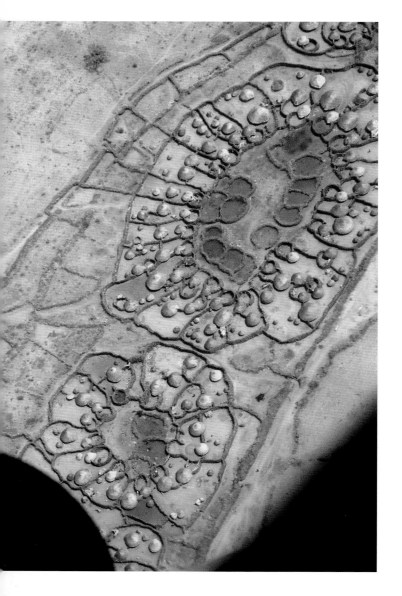

LEFT: An aerial view of a Karamojong village. The typical structure is clearly defensive, with a surrounding barrier made from roots and thorn branches. The darker area at the centre is where the cows are kept. Cows are the prized possessions of the community, and so they are kept safe within the circle of huts, as far away as possible from marauding neighbours.

RIGHT: A small boy peers out of the protective barrier encircling his village, observing our unexpected arrival with curiosity. It is only possible to enter a Karamojong village accompanied by someone who is known to them already. On this occasion our guide was Father Damian, the parish priest from the Comboni Missionaries in Matany. Without his help, it would have been impossible to take the photographs in this section of the book.

LEFT: Two men in the traditional robe worn by the people of Matany, a village in the most easterly part of Karamoja. In the Karamojong language, the word *ngimoe* means both 'enemy' and 'stranger', and foreigners are viewed with suspicion.

OPPOSITE: A young boy proudly displays his simple, but functional, weapons. Battles were once fought out with bows and arrows, but now people resort to gunfire. As a result, there are a significant number of casualties during raids on livestock, which the Karamojong consider a worthy and courageous activity that can earn them respect and honour.

LEFT: A young Karamojong lad, inseparable from his Kalashnikov.

RIGHT: A group of soldiers from the Ugandan army, sent from Kampala to impose a ceasefire in Karamoja. Every once in a while, the central authorities feel the need to flex their muscles in these regions. The Kalashnikovs disappear for a while, only to reappear when the army slackens its grip.

OVERLEAF: A herd drinking at a pool. The men enter the water with the animals and undress in order to have a wash. They are justly proud of their animals because the herd means everything to the Karamojong: wealth, prestige, dowry and goods that can be exchanged to cement alliances.

LEFT: An elderly man holding a wooden seat used either for sitting or as a headrest. This object is commonly found amongst nomadic and semi-nomadic peoples in East Africa. The only item of clothing worn is a simple robe.

RIGHT: A girl of marriageable age hides from the camera. The scarring on her forehead is traditionally thought to be a sign of beauty.

LEFT: A young boy on his way to visit the village witch in the hope that she will cure his stomach ache. His forehead has been painted, and he is carrying a lamb to be sacrificed during the rites of healing.

OPPOSITE: Tall and elegant, with simple coloured robes covering their naked bodies, the Karamojong are traditionally the most warlike people among all those who live along the course of the Nile. This young man is clutching a transistor radio and has tied attractive pieces of coloured string around his knees and his feet. All the young men take care of their appearance, often using recycled objects of Western origin as ornaments. The joints and washers from water pumps installed by humanitarian agencies are particularly fashionable.

OVERLEAF: At sunset a group of women return to their village, having fetched the necessary supply of water from the well.

CHAPTER TWO

Ethiopia: Christianity on the Blue Nile

PRECEDING PAGES: The cascades of Tis Isat on the Blue Nile. The waterfall, which is 45 metres high, is situated 30 kilometres beyond the point where the river branches off from Lake Tana.

OPPOSITE: A monk opens the wooden door of Saint George's Church (Beta Giorgis), situated on the Zege Peninsula on Lake Tana. It takes half an hour to travel there by boat from the small town of Bahir Dar. The Blue Nile is the principal distributary of the lake. Inside the church are ancient sacred paintings, which depict episodes from the Holy Scriptures.

ABOVE: A window of Beta Maryam church, Lalibela.

THE BLUE NILE IS KNOWN AS THE ABAY in Ethiopia and is 1,610 kilometres long. It springs from the mountains and after 750 metres reaches Lake Tana. Coursing south near the town of Bahir Dar, on the shore of Lake Tana, it carves the deepest canyon in Africa across the Ethiopian Plateau before entering Sudan. It then crosses the plains of Sennar, and at Khartoum merges with the other Nile, the White Nile, serving as its largest affluent. It is better known by the name of Blue Nile – blue like the colour of its limpid waters, unlike the muddy streams of its sister river.

We follow the Abay, with our feet on the muddy banks of Lake Tana, at an altitude of 1,788 metres. The distant sounds of tambourines echo in the humid and cloying dawn air, along with the tolling of bells and the subdued chanting of psalms. The sun does not seem eager to rise, and the darkness has thrown a cloak of pitch black over everything. At this time of day, Bahir Dar resembles a faded black-and-white film about ancient Christianity. Flurries of white veils can be seen disappearing in the direction of Saint George's Church, from which the sound of chanting emanates. In this lost corner of Africa faith lives on.

Hundreds of worshippers are lying prostrate on the ground inside and outside the church, quietly praying. A priest comes out of the church, bearing a large cross. Suddenly a long line forms – a mass of white figures kissing the sacred symbol. Christ is present, and He lives and flourishes as if the Gospel had been proclaimed only yesterday. Here, in one of the poorest countries in the world, faith is welcoming and inviting, and touches our hearts. The sound of the psalms being sung guides us towards the subterranean churches. The crowd is even denser now, and all the women are shrouded in white veils. The smell of damp earth mingles with the fragrance of various different herbs, and a few small hands reach out, begging. It is the morning mass – 'the most important one, the best one' according to a hermit, as he scuttles out of his grotto carved into the red rock.

We climb into the boat. On the horizon, the surface of the lake looks like a piece of foil – a mirror reflecting yellow and red light. A flock of pelicans soars up into the sky, watching the tiny fishing boats from way above. They are looking out for discarded fish. Christianity took refuge on this lake when the Nile regions were being invaded by Islam. The Gospel reached this place by following the course of the Nile backwards – from Palestine to Egypt, and then to the Ethiopian Plateau, far away from the great religious upheavals – and it has remained true to itself throughout two thousand years of history. The miracle of faith.

Now our boat is speeding along in a southerly direction, water lapping against banks covered with gigantic trees. There are thirty-seven islands on Lake Tana. A large number of ancient monasteries are hidden away on these islands, and are named after Christ, the Virgin and the Saints. They resemble medieval Gothic churches, where the stories of the Gospel were told through mosaics, as the population would have been illiterate. These are not the precious stained glass windows of Chartres but are brightly coloured pictures. The Saints feature predominantly, but many of them are unfamiliar to us.

We arrive on the island of Dek, where our helmsman prostrates himself (not merely on his knees, but on the ground) before Saint Michael, the judge of celestial souls. A priest picks up a branch to point out the illustrated scenes, one by one, like a storyteller: Saint George killing the dragon, Saint Raphael preventing a whale from destroying a church, Saint Yared teaching music to the birds, Saint Tekle Haymanot, who stood in prayer for seven years until he lost a leg, and the Madonna interceding at Judgment Day for the cannibal Belai. Belai was said to have eaten seventy-two people, but later repented, and offered water to a leper who begged to know his name. These stories are the encyclopaedia of popular Christianity.

We turn our backs on the islands and their monasteries, and head for the southern bank of Lake Tana. A small river snakes uncertainly through a marshy area of tall reeds. The boatman looks out intently for the silhouettes of hippopotamuses, but it is better to follow a small indentation in the bank that is drawing the waters towards itself. This is only a small river, perhaps a few dozen metres wide, but suddenly it expands out of all proportion to become the Blue Nile again. A few dozen kilometres further down the valley, it shows off its full strength, exploding down the waterfall of Tis Isat. At 45 metres high, it is the second largest waterfall in Africa. From here, the Nile flows on through the fissure it has carved out over the millennia: a long gorge that forms a sweeping curve around the Goggiam Mountains. Then it drops steeply down towards the fertile Sudanese plains.

A village on the plateau that stretches away above Lalibela, at an altitude of 4,000 metres. From here a tortuous mountain path leads to the monastery of Asheton Maryam.

LEFT: One of the golden crosses from the treasury of Narga Selassie monastery, on the island of Dek, almost at the centre of the lake. Fleeing the Arab incursions and the enforcement of Islam, Orthodox Christianity took refuge here on the Ethiopian Plateau, where its age-old traditions have been maintained.

OPPOSITE: One of the sacred texts from Narga Selassie. The monks are proud to display their sacred treasures, in return for a small offering. Inhabitants around the lake are much more assertive, pestering Western visitors for money and peddling their homemade articles with great insistence.

Interiors of Christian monasteries in Ethiopia are covered with biblical scenes. Alongside the familiar stories, there are tales from local folklore featuring Ethiopian saints.

OPPOSITE: One of the many images of Saint George in Narga Selassie monastery. As he is the patron saint of Ethiopia, images of Saint George are predominant in the country's churches. He appears either as king of the saints or on his horse, slaying the dragon. Stories about Belai, the cannibal who converted to Christianity on his deathbed, are also frequently depicted.

RIGHT: The iconostasis at the church of Beta Maryam, on the Zege Peninsula, Lake Tana. A monk prepares to open the magnificent doors to the high altar, where mass is to be celebrated.

LEFT: An unexpected encounter near the Tis Isat waterfall on the Blue Nile. A bride, her face covered, is carried on a donkey to the marriage ceremony, where the bridegroom is waiting. Her slight figure suggests that she may be very young. As in many parts of Africa, marriages are decided by the families of the couple. The relatives sing and dance.

RIGHT: Another group of people fire shots into the air with old shotguns to celebrate the happy occasion.

OVERLEAF: A glimpse of the Blue Nile beyond the Tis Isat waterfall. The boats used by the fishermen, known as *tankwa*, bear a striking similarity to depictions in pharaonic tombs and temples.

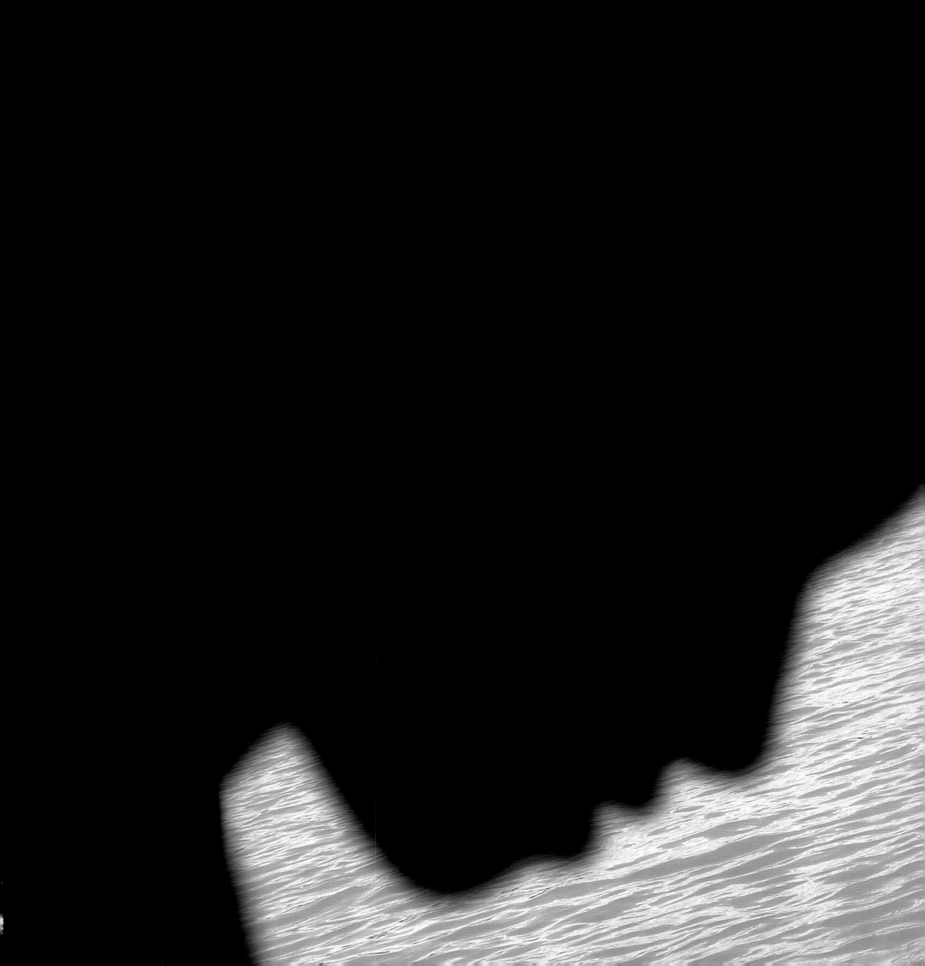

OPPOSITE: A man heads towards the market at Bahir Dar, laden with chickens. Peasants from the surrounding countryside walk for several hours in order to reach the city, where they can sell their wares and buy the essentials.

RIGHT: A woman on her way to the first mass of the day at Bahir Dar, carrying her baby on her back.

With Lake Tana behind us, we begin to climb steeply between chains of mountains. Their silhouettes strike terror into the heart. Lalibela lies hidden at an altitude of 2,700 metres – a village made up of straw-thatched huts, known as *tukuls,* and huts of mud and straw. To me it seems that this place equates to the Vatican of the Orthodox Ethiopian religion. There is a whole network of underground churches dug out of the red volcanic rock, a huge excavation enterprise begun in the thirteenth century. In those days it would have been a colossal undertaking. During the daily celebrations of mass, and on the special church festival days, myriads of worshippers throng these underground passages, which connect the churches and their forecourts. The crowd is devout, prostrated in prayer on the ground, like the first-century Christians hidden away in the catacombs.

The door to this world is opened for us by Father Estifanos. With skin blacker than night, he is the guardian of the keys to the treasury in the church of Bet Meskel. Within a few minutes, rays of sunshine are illuminating a dazzling array of silver and gold crosses, studded with precious jewels. Some of the oldest crosses have four arms of equal length, enclosed by a circle. At the base, there is a representation of the tabernacle, containing the Ark of the Covenant, which according to the tradition of the Ethiopian church was stolen by Menelik I – traditionally believed to be the son of the Queen of Sheba and King Solomon – and brought into Ethiopia. A safe haven was sought for it on one of the islands on Lake Tana, Tana Kirkos, and from here the Ark is said to have been transported to Axum, where it is still believed to reside. Estifanos has greasy, unkempt hair, dirty hands and muddy clothing. He and his fellow monks live in a series of miserable mud huts, in abject poverty. They live on what they can produce on their vegetable patch. It is not an easy life, and few would choose to lead it. Maybe Christ himself lived like that, just like Estifanos.

The underground church of Medhane Alem at Lalibela, the night before the Orthodox Easter. A crowd of worshippers has arrived from the surrounding villages, thronging into the church. The heat makes it almost impossible to breathe. At midnight the candles are lit, and the priests begin to celebrate the paschal liturgy. Medhane Alem is carved out of rock and is believed to be the largest church of its kind in the world.

LEFT: The entrance to the church of Beta Maryam is reached via an underground gallery from Medhane Alem. Covered passageways and tunnels interconnect an astonishing eleven different churches carved out of rock at Lalibela, which is reminiscent of Petra in Jordan.

OPPOSITE: Two young women dressed in the white robes traditionally worn for liturgical celebrations.

OVERLEAF: The upper section of one of the most spectacular churches in Lalibela, the church of Saint George (Beta Giorgis). The excavation work that uncovered the main structure of this church is clearly visible.

LEFT: A woman working in the fields proudly displays the crucifix she wears around her neck. The first Christian preachers arrived in Ethiopia in the fourth century, teaching the Monophysite doctrine – the belief that the nature of Christ was purely divine, rather than human and divine. These *ante litteram* missionaries arrived at the court of the Axumite Empire and converted the king, who initiated a campaign to disseminate the new faith. Monasteries spread like wildfire, making Ethiopia one of the first Christian kingdoms. Hidden away in a chapel in Axum, which nobody is allowed to enter, there are stone tablets; Ethiopians believe them to be the Ten Commandments that God gave to Moses on Mount Sinai, miraculously transported to the Ethiopian Plateau in the Ark of the Covenant.

RIGHT: Priests at the celebration of an Orthodox liturgy. The most important of these are Leddet (Christmas) and Timkat (Epiphany).

OVERLEAF: A monk reading his breviary in a niche carved out of the rock, which serves as a resting place.

CHAPTER THREE

Sudan: The White Nile Rediscovered

BEYOND THE UGANDAN BORDER, the White Nile merges with the waters of the Aswa River and starts to spread across the vast Sudanese savannah. This huge, flat plain has only recently ceased to be ravaged by a civil war, which raged for over twenty years. It has commonly been defined as a conflict between the Arab Muslims of the north and the Christians of the south, fighting for their independence. But the truth is much more complex than that, as it involves not just religious issues, but also ancestral tensions.

'It is true that we are Christians, and that we do not want to be under Sharia Law, but we are also fighting for our human rights,' declares Zakaria Odong, leader of an army camp of rebel troops near Wau. Shortly beforehand he had subjected me to a harsh interrogation because I had entered the territory he controlled without a permit. He explained his point of view in impeccable English: 'We want liberty – Khartoum has no right to decide for us simply because we are black and they are Arab.'

In 2005 a peace treaty granted the southern rebels autonomy for six years, but according to estimates the war had resulted in more than two million deaths as well as the displacement of over four million people. As if that were not enough, the fragile peace is based on a pipe dream – a dream of oil, which Sudan has in abundance, so much so in fact that both the Chinese and the Americans have arrived there with the intent of drilling in the savannah. Who knows whether any dollars will ever trickle down to the people....

On entering Sudan, the river bathes the beleaguered city of Juba, the fortress belonging to the armed troops of John Garang, the former leader of the Sudan People's Liberation Army, or SPLA, who died in a helicopter accident in 2005. A few kilometres further downstream, the banks of the river become increasingly indistinct. This is the start of the Sudd, an Arabic word meaning 'barrier'. From here on, for several hundred kilometres, the river widens out unrecognizably, and loses itself in a vast flood plain that can cover an area of over 130,000 square kilometres in the wet season. The great river divides into a myriad of indistinguishable and tortuous channels. At such a width, half of its water is lost through evaporation, and the river becomes a marsh, covered with water hyacinths and a sea of papyrus plants. It is a prime habitat for wild animals: hippopotamuses, crocodiles and white-eared kob, a breed of antelope. Before the war, this area had the highest concentration of mammals per square kilometre in the whole of Africa, but now the great herds are a distant memory.

Two million people live in the Sudd. Many are Dinka, Nuer, Shilluk and nomads, mostly Fellata. Their cows are their greatest source of pride. Belonging to the Nilotic-Hamitic race, they are very proud peoples, bound tightly to their traditions. They are warriors too: John Garang was a Dinka, as were most of the members of the SPLA.

Shortly before reaching Malakal, the Nile emerges from the swamps to flow along a riverbed. Yet the river still cannot be contained: during the rainy season it bursts its banks, and the flooding can have disastrous consequences. Firstly, it merges with the waters of the Gazelle River, then with the waters of the Sobat, and then it navigates a determined course north, across the stunning African savannah, which becomes increasingly arid. Along the great river there is life in abundance.

The Shilluk fishermen build their villages of mud huts under the large baobab trees, which offer shade from the sun. The king of this people lives in Kodok (Fashoda), in a very unusual castle made completely of mud and woven straw. Soldiers armed with Kalashnikovs patrol the entrance. This is a volatile area, under the control of former rebels from the SPLA. Not far away, on the other side of the Nile, the official Sudanese army of government forces has control. Peace has consolidated the geographical positions of the various military groups. When the peace treaty expires, a referendum for independence is scheduled to be held.

Finally we reach Khartoum, the capital of Sudan. Here the White Nile and the Blue Nile join together in a passionate embrace. For several kilometres, the muddier waters of the White Nile refuse to mingle with the greener waters of its sister, the Blue Nile, which has descended from the Ethiopian Plateau. Khartoum is a pivotal point in Africa, for it is here that it mingles with the Arabic world, the Gospel confronts the Koran. It has been like this for centuries, ever since the days of the great Omdurman market, trading in ivory, spices and slaves – around 50,000 annually before the slave trade was abolished. Today, the city resembles a giant melting pot. Development has catapulted it towards modernity, but it is held back by religious intransigence bubbling away beneath the surface. On the streets of the capital, wealth and poverty live side by side; powerful cars drive past starving refugees from the south, and from the most recent conflicts in western Darfur.

This couple, encountered along the Nile in the Kaka area, were pleased to pose for a photograph, if a little amazed.

OVERLEAF: A nomad family leads its flock of goats and a few camels to drink from the waters of the Nile.

LEFT: A group of boys at Waddakona play in the branches of the large trees that make the Nile so verdant here. It's a tranquil setting, but numerous roadblocks along the tracks are a constant reminder of the war that ravaged the area. The territory is still marked like the spots on a leopard, with some patches controlled by government forces and others by ex-rebels from the SPLA (Sudan People's Liberation Army).

RIGHT: Not far from Malakal, a large herd of oxen are quenching their thirst in the waters of the Nile. The nomads come down to the river in the morning, and then retire to the savannah when the heat becomes fierce, taking their animals with them to graze. The boys take the opportunity to wash themselves, before returning to their main activity, acting as shepherds looking after the beasts.

LEFT: A village in the Nuba Mountains. During the recent civil war, the Nuba people, who are partly Christian, took refuge in the mountains to escape the attacks of the government forces. Today, the route into the mountains is still littered with unexploded mines. It will take years to clear the area. Famous for combat, the Nuba were immortalized in the 1960s by the German photographer Leni Riefenstahl. Since those days, their customs have completely changed, as the war destroyed all their traditions. The war has also affected the peace-loving nature of the other peoples in the vast territory known as the Sudd: the Dinka, the Nuer and the Shilluk.

RIGHT: A young Shilluk man, armed with spears and an axe, returns from a market in one of the villages along the Nile.

OVERLEAF: A group of boys jumping into the water from the banks of one of the Nile's canals, close to a small rural settlement called Keri Kera.

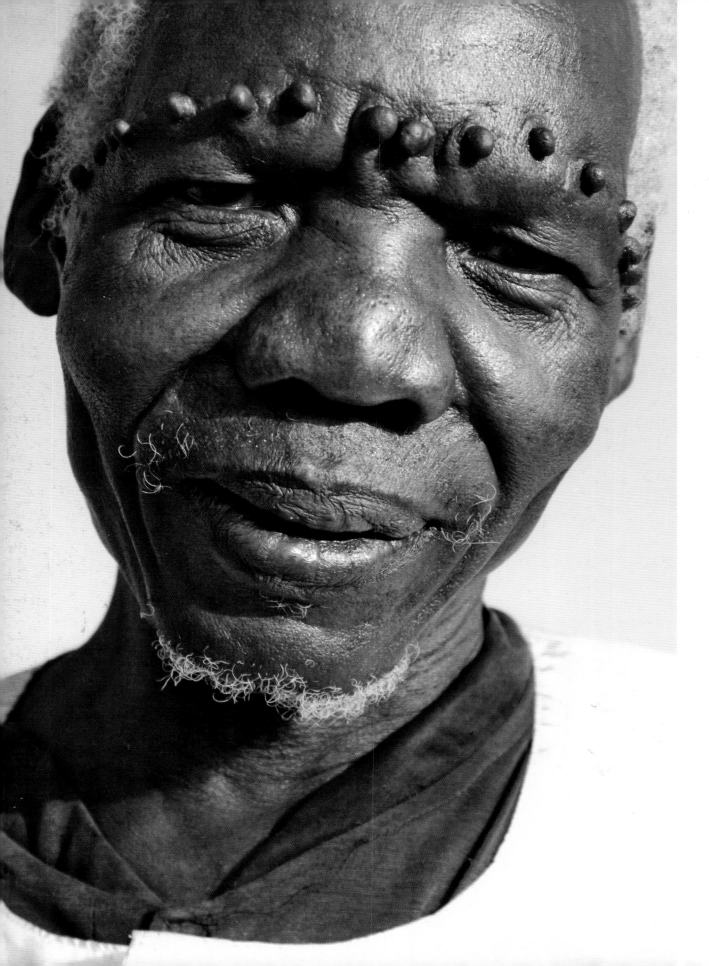

LEFT: This Shilluk man has an unusual type of tattoo on his forehead, a custom that is now dying out as parents choose against putting their own children through the process – a further sign of how traditional customs in southern Sudan are changing.

RIGHT: A group of Shilluk from Kodok, the seat of their sovereign. Dozens of peoples are under his control, inhabiting the vast area between the Nuba Mountains and the Nile. In order to reach the town, you have to get past a roadblock controlled by the ex-rebels of the SPLA.

OPPOSITE: People dive into the river at Kodok to cool down during the hottest time of the day. A boat shuttles between the two sides of the river, carrying people who are cultivating plots of land on the fertile banks of the Nile. During the recent civil war, most of the towns along the Nile were in the hands of the army from Khartoum. These days, foreigners who make it this far are regarded with a great deal of suspicion and subjected to stringent police checks. Photography is virtually impossible.

RIGHT: There are numerous children along the banks of the Nile. Most of them fish and seem to play very few games. The tough life here forces them to participate in the daily chores of family life from an early age.

LEFT: The desert track along the left bank of the Nile from Kosti is not frequented by many motor vehicles, just a few lorries bursting at the seams with people and produce. The surface of the road is very rough and becomes impassable during the rainy season when the river bursts its banks. Even when conditions are favourable it still takes almost four days to travel the 520 kilometres between Kosti and Malakal, the largest city in the south.

RIGHT: In a village along the Nile a small boy works alongside his parents, filling his family's small grain store with millet. The grain store is like a big cask made from banco, a mixture of mud and straw. When it has been filled up, the precious storage tower is closed over at the top with a conical roof made of straw.

LEFT: The shipyard at Khartoum, on the banks of the Nile. Ancient methods are still used to saw the planks of wood, which are then utilized to build feluccas.

RIGHT: The spectacularly colourful market at Omdurman, one of the liveliest markets in East Africa. This is in the most conservative part of the town, where the Sufis are seen every Friday evening outside their mosques. The Sufis conquered Khartoum in 1885, after an epic battle during which the English general Charles Gordon lost his life, having been at the forefront of those defending the town. The Sufis were led by a Muslim religious leader called Muhammad Ahmad (1844–85), a self-proclaimed Mahdi and advocate of jihad, the holy war against the occupying force of the Turko-Egyptian administration which was in power in Sudan in those days. Today, the tomb of the Mahdi has become a destination for pilgrims.

OVERLEAF: A young boy washes on the banks of the Blue Nile near Khartoum. The clothes on the bushes have just been washed by his sister and have been put out to dry.

CHAPTER FOUR

Sudan: The Nile Traverses
the Nubian Desert

NOW WE HAVE LEFT THE SUDANESE CAPITAL BEHIND US. After the grand embrace of the sister rivers, the great river becomes solemn, grandiose. Having lapped at the banks of Khartoum and flowed under the bridges that span the two sides, the Nile slashes across the desert like a glinting blade. The bridges are controlled by armed police. Daring to take a single photograph could get us into a lot of trouble with the authorities. Anyone who did so would have his roll of film confiscated. The police presence in Sudan is pervasive and obsessive. Even in the most remote villages a plain clothes policeman will turn up, arrogantly demanding to see documents and travel permits. And again, no photography is allowed. Westerners are questioned on sight, but told it is only for their own safety. It is certainly not pleasant to travel under such scrutiny.

It is dawn, and although the sun is still low in the sky, it makes our eyes hurt as it bathes the flat, stony desert in light. Sand and rocks; yellow and ochre; silence and the absolute nothingness of the landscape. The Nile heads north and enters the Nubian Desert, the ancient region that historically extended beyond Egypt, as far as Aswan.

This is a forgotten land, yet rich in history and archaeology. The sand has buried precious traces of ancient civilizations, mythical cities, Ptolemaic palaces, tombs and early Christian churches – and of course the pyramids that call to mind the Nubian pharaohs of the 25th dynasty, who dominated Egypt between c. 800 and 657 BC from their capital at Napata.

The final king of the 25th dynasty, Tantamani, was forced by the Assyrians to withdraw to Napata, and Egyptian rule passed to Psamtek I. The royal bloodline of the 25th dynasty lived on, however, in Upper Nubia for another 350 years, in a kingdom that stretched from the first cataract to the White Nile. The border between the two kingdoms, which is now submerged beneath the waters of Lake Nasser, remained in existence throughout the Ptolemaic and Roman eras. Today, reminders of these historic events emerge here and there along the course of the Nile.

The yellow of the sand, the blue of the Nile, and the green of the palm groves curving down towards the riverbank. Here, the great river is like a pulsing artery. A source of provision. Its waters are channels of communication – at least until the rapids interrupt the flow. Between Khartoum and Aswan there are six classical cataracts (although the second is now submerged in the waters of Lake Nasser), impressive jets of water and rapids that make navigation difficult. Between the fifth and the sixth cataracts the ancient royal city of Meroë rises out of the sand, founded in the eighth century BC. Rich and powerful, it once encompassed an area of several dozen square kilometres. The important temple of Amun was once situated here, a gigantic construction that housed a sacred pool, fed by the water of the Nile. A solitary sequence of pyramid-shaped tombs rises up outside the city, amidst the sand dunes. This is Nubia in all its glory: a picture-postcard of times long past and yet unchanged, with the Bedouin on their camels, disappearing into the horizon of red sand.

The river flows on, and the desert continues. This time we are crossing the Bayuda Desert, a vast expanse delineated by the bend of the river along the fourth, fifth and sixth cataracts. Only close to the water's edge does the desert show some clemency, allowing the cultivation of small pockets of land for corn, wheat and tomatoes; small flashes of green set against the volcanic rocks and the vast expanses of wadis, the dried-up riverbeds. Far from the river, there are nomads tending herds of camel and flocks of sheep, leading them to remote wells. They are always in search of that most precious commodity: water. They resemble biblical scenes, a way of life that has remained unchanged for centuries. It is relentlessly hot, reaching forty-five degrees in summer, and the sun blazes mercilessly on.

Now we are getting ready to cross the Nile. We are waiting for a run-down ferry, which harks back to the English colonial era. There is a large crowd: women laden with fruit and vegetables, men in white caftans leading flocks of sheep, herds of camels, rusty off-road vehicles, carts pulled by donkeys and small vans. The crowd presses in tightly. The motor is running at full speed to overcome the force of the great river's impetuous current. Finally we reach Karima, and the striking red sandstone cliff-face of the sacred mountain of Gebel Barkal, the site of a great temple dedicated to the god Amun. This place was the Olympia of the Nubian pharaohs, and for thousands of years it was the capital and the religious heart of Nubia. A long row of granite rams marks the path of an ancient road that most likely led to a wharf on the banks of the Nile.

Mosques silhouetted against the sunset sky near Karima.

OVERLEAF: The pyramids at the ancient city of Meroë, which flourished from c. 300 BC to c. AD 360.

LEFT: A group of boys quenching their thirst in an irrigation channel, which has been diverted from the main course of the river in order to irrigate the plots of land being cultivated near the fourth cataract.

OPPOSITE: Women loading a boat on the Nile, close to Old Dongola.

OVERLEAF: Camels and men disembarking from the Nile ferry at Ad-Dabbah. This is a necessary part of the journey for anyone travelling north up the Nile. A long wait should always be expected as there is always a melee of motor vehicles, camels, donkeys and men – and so much dust that it seems as if the air has been liberally sprinkled with puffs of talcum powder.

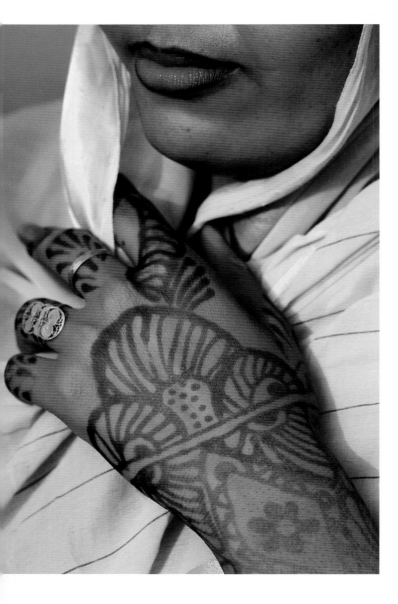

LEFT: A woman from Korti, her hands painted with henna. After traversing the desert, the Nile assumes the aspect of a much longed-for oasis, where there is a chance of encountering civilization once more.

RIGHT: A couple of camels lean on their owner's shoulder. In Egypt, camels – or rather dromedaries, to be more accurate – have been relegated to a marginal role, whereas in Sudan they are used much more widely, particularly as a means of transport. Without them, the nomads would not survive, as they wander around from place to place with their animals in search of meagre pasture and isolated water sources.

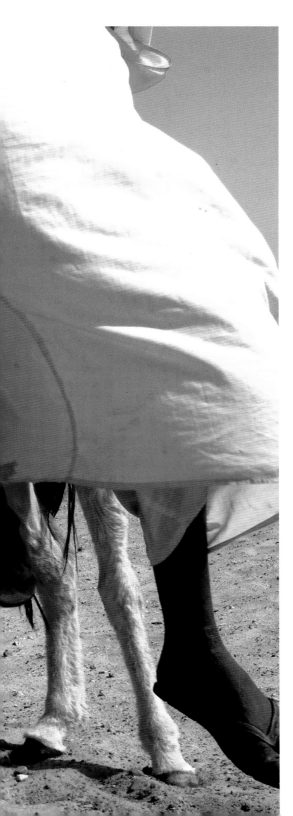

After Karima, the villages along the Nile seem frozen in time. There is a series of small groups of habitations, which have nothing in common with the urban chaos and filth of the cities. We enter an ancient world, where life is simple; where the faces of children light up in amazement when they see a white visitor; where the women hide shyly from the camera lens, but throw open their doors to welcome a guest into their home and offer a moment's respite from the relentless heat. Here there is generous Arab hospitality, and it is truly a pleasure to quench one's thirst with a refreshing cup of tea.

RIGHT: Two men draw together for a photograph, proud of their close friendship.

LEFT: A view of the Nile from the sacred mountain of Gebel Barkal, where there are ruins of a great temple dedicated to the god Amun.

RIGHT: The papyrus plant, which was first known to have been used by the ancient Egyptians, is abundant along the banks of the Nile in Sudan and Uganda but has almost disappeared in Egypt, mostly because of pollution. The triangular stem, which grows to a height of between three and five metres, culminates in a profuse bunch of fronds.

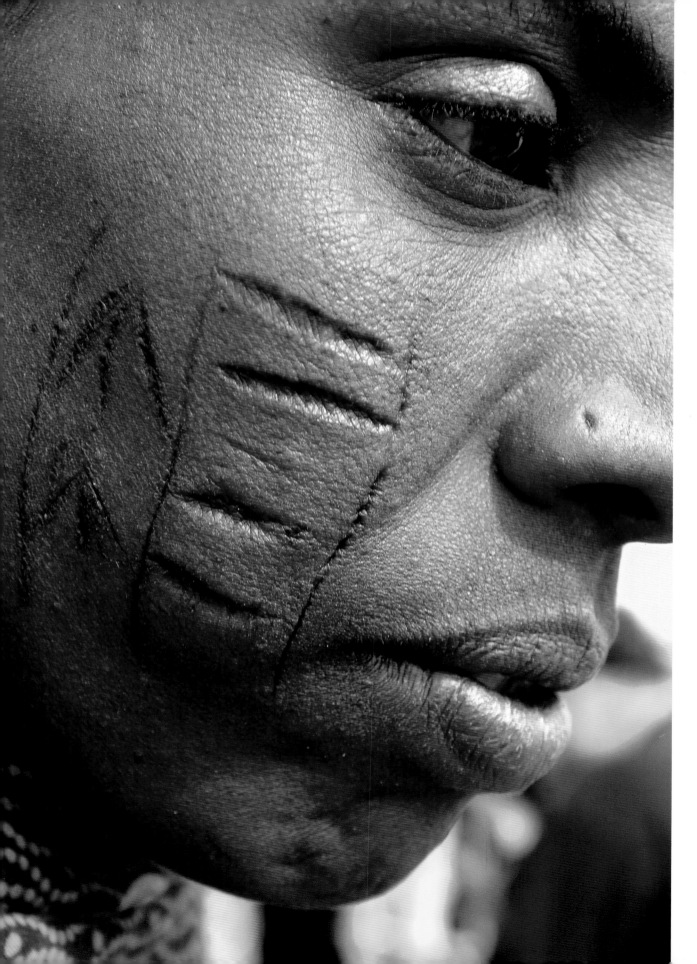

LEFT: In the Wadi el-Milk area, not far from the Nile, a woman displays the deep scars on her cheek, which show that she belongs to the Kababish nomads.

OPPOSITE: Collecting water near Musawwarat al-Sufrah. Wells are essential to the existence of the nomads living in the desert, whose movements are governed by the need to find precious supplies of water. When they find a well, the animals are watered, and they fill up their cans and girba, goatskin water bags. If the well is especially deep, they use camels to help draw the water up; otherwise the task falls to the youngsters or even the women. No distinction is made between the sexes, despite the arduous nature of the work.

Downstream from Gebel Barkal, there is a simple collection of houses on the banks of the Nile. El-Kurru is the site of the necropolis of the ancient city of Napata, and it is thought that the Napatan kings' residence lay nearby, although it has never been found. The tombs bear a close resemblance to the royal pyramids in Egypt. More sand: the Nile widens out between the dunes, bay after bay resembling seashores surrounded by solitary mountains; then a few sudden patches of green – small oases; chromatic leaps in the dazzling yellow of the sand. It continues like this until Old Dongola, where a rocky, 50-metre-high cliff face towers over the Nile. The ruins of two Christian temples emerge from the sand. There are columns and capitals, decorated with Orthodox crosses dating from the tenth and eleventh centuries AD, when Nubia – bearing the name of the kingdom of Makuria – became a Christian state that resisted the Arab invasion.

There are more villages, with snow-white houses nestling in the shade of the palm trees, which can be reached by sandy tracks that run along the banks of the Nile, sometimes disappearing inland, into the parched and sun-drenched interior. Each new scene is one of order and cleanliness. The houses are built of clay, with roofs made from palm fronds or acacia branches, surrounded and enclosed by a high boundary wall. The gateways are truly magnificent, all painted with wonderful designs using strong colours, kaleidoscopic decorations, geometric or chequered patterns, and figurative images. Sometimes the walls of the houses are also painted with a mixture of symbols from traditional and Islamic culture, such as the pilgrimage to Mecca, camels, snakes or crocodiles. The mixture of images is fantastical and bizarre, but there are also stories about everyday folk on the walls, windows into the common man's way of life.

Wadi Halfa lies on the Sudanese border. Egypt awaits us, and the vast Lake Nasser, where the Nile widens out beyond recognition.

This type of decoration is typical of the Nubian houses near the Egyptian border, which are characterized by multi-coloured decorations on gateways and walls. Fantastical geometric designs, lines, dots and circles are often incorporated.

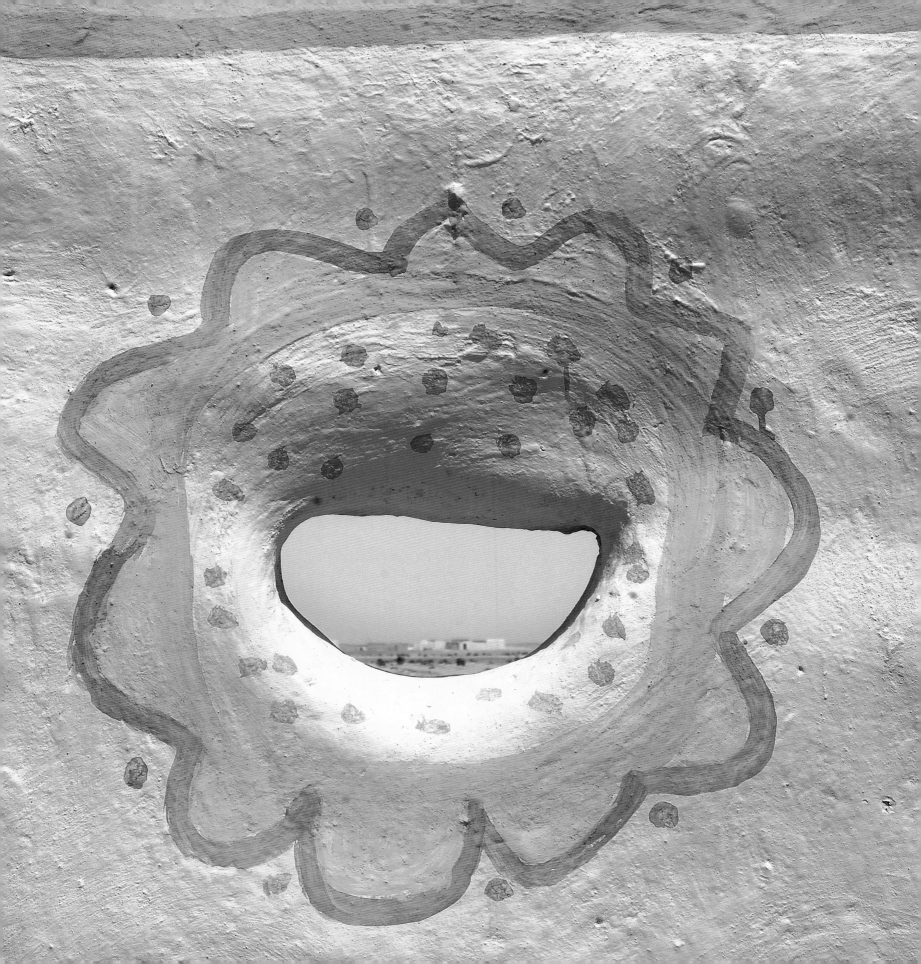

LEFT: A crocodile head above the door of a Nubian house. According to popular belief, the animal will keep all perils at bay.

RIGHT: The painted entrance to the courtyard of a house, which is built in the typical style found north of Dongola.

A man and a woman from the remote village of Kerma. The friendliness of the inhabitants is reflected in their smiles.

OVERLEAF: Painted houses north of Kerma. The women are hiding from the camera behind the walls of the houses. The courtyard has been painstakingly decorated with a large chequerboard design.

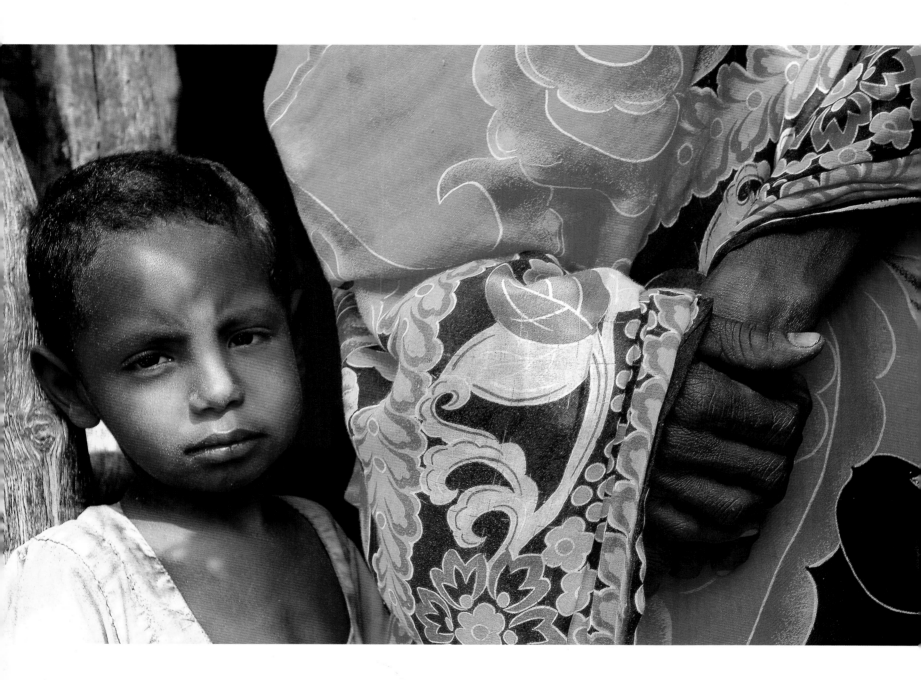

OPPOSITE: A boy clings to his mother, fearful of the approaching camera. She tries to reassure him, unsuccessfully.

RIGHT: A woman carries a frugal meal into the desert, where her sons are shepherding their flocks of goats in the pastures along the Nile.

OVERLEAF: Small family plots of land exploit the fertile ground along the fourth cataract of the Nile.

CHAPTER FIVE

Egypt of the Pharaohs:
The Glory of the Nile

PRECEDING PAGES: The temple of the pharaoh Ramesses II at Abu Simbel, in the evening. When the water level of the Nile rose due to the construction of the Aswan Dam, UNESCO set about reconstructing the temple piece by piece to prevent it from being submerged by the waters of Lake Nasser. Salvage work began in 1964. Forty million dollars was spent dismantling two monuments – one dedicated to Ramesses II and Ra, the other to Hathor – which were cut into large chunks and reassembled 65 metres higher.

OPPOSITE: A man climbs the mast of a felucca to unfurl the sails before setting off from Aswan harbour.

ABOVE: The image of a prisoner carved onto the entrance of the temple of Ramesses II at Abu Simbel.

FROM THE DAL CATARACT IN SUDAN TO ASWAN IN EGYPT, the great river is transformed into a vast artificial lake, closed off by two dams at Aswan. Lake Nasser was created by the construction of the Aswan High Dam, built across the Nile to control the river's annual floods. However, the dam caused the water level along Lake Nasser to rise by nearly 100 metres, and not only did several hundred thousand people see their villages disappear under water, but many ancient Nubian treasures were at risk of being lost forever. Several important Nubian temples and monuments were dismantled and transported to a higher location, safely above the water level, most notably Abu Simbel.

It takes three days to cross this vast expanse of Nile. There is total silence all around. The banks of the river lack vegetation, and the mountains stand as stark silhouettes against the horizon. The desert seems never-ending. As in the depths of the Sahara, the dawn and the sunset are truly cinematic, with the breeze rippling the gilded surface of the water. Once on dry land, there are a few more kilometres to be covered on foot through the nothingness, in search of the temples that have been rescued. We feel like the first people to have stumbled on the large overturned statue of Ramesses II, which lies in the sand in the Valley of the Lions, where a line of sphinxes guards the temple of Wadi el-Sebua. Each temple is a surprise, and not just in terms of archaeology.

At Hamada a young lad appears. He has a baby crocodile in his hands. I wonder where he found it. He maintains that the young reptiles are found in the fishermen's nets, and has come here for a photograph. 'Baksheesh, please,' he says: he wants a tip, but not in euros because there is nowhere to change money. There is no bank here in the desert. It would only be a mirage....

'Mister! Señor! Monsieur! Please, tour in felucca....' Walking along the corniche, which winds along the right bank of the Nile, visitors are easy prey for hawkers. Since the time of the pharaohs, Aswan has been the greatest commercial emporium of the whole Upper Nile Valley, strategically placed for trade between the Mediterranean and equatorial Africa. The heart of the ancient city was on Elephantine Island, not far from the first cataract, a natural barrier impeding navigation. Our boat crosses the Nile again, and moors alongside the jetty on the island of Sehel. The villages are typically Nubian – ochre, red and blue, unremittingly strong colours. There are murals like abstract paintings, and decorations and tracery reminiscent of Sudan. Our feet sink into the sand.

Young Ahmed runs to meet us. He sells little boxes, galabiyyas, necklaces, bracelets, and if desired he also hires out camels and donkeys, or so he says, with all the authority that his eight years of age can muster. We need only ask, and he will get it for us. To remain within four walls is impossible when the sky is always blue, and the waters of the Nile so cool and inviting. What fun it is to take a dip in the river with his friends. 'Nile good,' he says. His brilliant white teeth gleam in the sunlight, and his clear blue eyes are shining, contrasting with his bronzed skin. Who knows what mixed blood may be coursing through his veins. It is said that in this region, at the furthermost edge of their empire, the Romans left behind an entire legion and their families, perhaps as a customs post en route to the heart of Africa – a people that saved itself from the Arab invasions. Today it re-emerges in the colour of eyes, or in red or blond hair.

To reach Sehel from Aswan, the rapids flow upstream between huge blocks of granite, smoothed by the force of the great river. We pass islets, rocks and feluccas in full sail. The bays, coves and gorges are reminiscent of the coast, but this is the Nile; it is freshwater, not saltwater, so the camels come down to the banks to drink from it. There are tiny golden beaches with fine sand, clearly sand from the desert. We have now reached the two dams. The first one, the lower one, was constructed in 1902; the larger one was completed in 1970 and is 111 metres high. They stand like swords firmly planted in the middle of the Nile. The landscape changed dramatically as a result, not only in archaeological terms. While the old dam only altered the flow of the Nile, the new one has put a stop to the annual flooding, which since the days of the pharaohs had always been such a blessing for agriculture. Today, without the benefit of the river silt, the local people are forced to resort to chemical fertilizers, although the dam does supply Egypt with a good supply of electricity.

A camel on the banks of the Nile near the first cataract. Once indispensable for travelling around the desert, camels have now been displaced by motor vehicles and in Egypt have increasingly been restricted to use in tourism. At Aswan, trips are offered on the back of a camel, along the banks of the Nile as far as the first of the two great dams on Lake Nasser.

LEFT: A felucca ploughs through the waters of the Nile near Aswan. The desert sand comes right down to the riverbank. After the yellow of the desert, the waters of the great river soothe the spirits with their calm blue hues, and soften the glare of the white light, which cuts like the blade of a knife.

RIGHT: A detail from the Kiosk of Qertassi, which is located close to the second great dam on the Nile. This precious relic of the Roman era has also been dismantled and reconstructed, to save it from the waters of Lake Nasser.

OVERLEAF: Sailing along the Nile near Aswan. A series of islands of varying sizes serve as a warning, heralding the granite rocks and the rapids of the first cataract, which stretch for about five kilometres. After negotiating all these obstacles, we reach the first great dam on the river, which was constructed in 1902.

Wadi el-Sebua Temple, also known as 'the Valley of the Lions', was dismantled and reconstructed in order to save it from the waters of Lake Nasser. A fallen statue of Ramesses II has been left on the ground by the archaeologists, perhaps to give the impression that things are exactly as they were before the relocation. The temples of el-Dakka and el-Maharraqa are visible on the horizon. To the left, the line of sphinxes that stretches along the Nile.

OVERLEAF: Elephantine Island, once the ancient heart of Aswan, and the southernmost border town during the pharaonic era. It was the most important city in Ancient Egypt, and was then known as Ibu, which means elephant, a clear reference to the ivory trade coming from central Africa. It is 1,500 metres in length and contains many archaeological ruins. There are two Nubian villages in the interior of the island, with brightly coloured houses. Next to Elephantine Island is Kitchener Island – named after its first owner, a British general – which is now a botanical garden.

The Corniche, which runs along the banks of the Nile at Aswan, and market stalls, where there are traditionally many different spices to choose from. Further upstream from the first cataract, between the two Aswan dams, is the site of Philae, one of the pearls of Ancient Egypt. This island on the Nile, whose temples have also been dismantled and reconstructed to save them from submersion, has been a sacred place since time immemorial: 'Philae' means 'island of the reign of Ra', the sun god and the most important deity in the Egyptian pantheon. For thousands of years it was a centre of worship of the goddess Isis, a maternal deity, wife of Osiris and mother of Horus. Even in Christian times, up until the advent of Islam in the seventh century, newly married women would go to the temple dedicated to the goddess and scratch some dust off its walls to take home, in order to ensure pregnancy. In the first years of the Christian era, Isis was associated with the Virgin Mary. In ancient times it was thought that the source of the Nile was beneath the island and its waters gushed forth from an underground cave where Hapy, the god of the Nile, lived.

The Nubian village of Sehel, on Sehel Island, not far from the old Aswan Dam. The walls of the village are painted in the typical Nubian style, very similar to those found in the Nubian villages in Sudan. Many stone tablets from the pharaonic era have been found on the island. The most important find, the Famine Stela, purports to be a record of famine in the time of Djoser (*c.* 2600 BC) but is thought to be Ptolemaic (after 332 BC).

OVERLEAF: Boys try to cross a branch of the Nile on the back of a reluctant donkey.

The people in this area are Egyptian, but more importantly they are Nubian, speaking an ancient language that has its roots in Meroïtic script. The Nubians are an aboriginal people who existed before the Arab invasions and, like the Copts (the Egyptian Christians), are among the most ancient peoples on earth. Moreover, the Nubian Christians are the most direct descendants of the ancient civilization of the Nubian pharaohs (25th dynasty).

Aswan is an enclosed territory: the Nubian Desert lies to the south and Egypt to the north, a land steeped in myth and the grandiose history of the pharaohs. It takes three days to travel by boat along the stretch of the Nile between Aswan and Luxor. There is an impressive succession of temples at Kom Ombo, Edfu and Esna, with their imposing complexes on the Nile. Some people choose to travel this stretch on a cruise liner, with every possible comfort and air-conditioning in the summer, when the temperature reaches over forty degrees. There are others who content themselves with a rather more spartan felucca, sleeping on the banks of the river, just as in ancient times – when Egypt had not yet been violated, when the temples of Karnak and Luxor still lay in sand-covered oblivion. The Valley of the Kings was desecrated by predators: grave robbers who plundered the treasure as a source of lucrative trade with collectors and museums. What took place then was nothing short of smuggling, masquerading as archaeological studies.

A small boy hidden in the back of a calash which is heading for the temple of Horus at Edfu, a few hundred metres away from the banks of the Nile.

OPPOSITE: A detail from the mortuary temple of Queen Hatshepsut at Deir el-Bahri, near Luxor. The colossal statues merge into the limestone crags. The temple complex is composed of many different terraces and is partially carved into the rock. It is extremely beautiful, but was defaced by Hatshepsut's successor, Thutmose III, who hated the queen and obliterated her image and her cartouche wherever they occurred.

RIGHT: A multi-coloured detail from Medinet Habu, the mortuary temple of Ramesses III, which is located near Luxor. This imposing building was built on an earlier temple dedicated to Amun. In its heyday, Medinet Habu was not only a place of worship, but also the administrative centre of ancient Thebes.

LEFT: The temple of Horus at Edfu, the most imposing and well-preserved of all the Egyptian temples, was constructed in the Ptolemaic Period in several stages and was completed in the first century BC. Falcon-headed god Horus, son of Osiris, killed his uncle, the god Seth, in revenge for the murder of his own father. The temple is said to stand on the site of the fight between the two gods.

OPPOSITE: Detail from the temple of Kom Ombo, dedicated to crocodile-headed god Sobek and Haroeris (Horus the Elder). The building is situated on a promontory of the Nile, on a curve of the river, and offers a wonderful view of feluccas, stretching as far as the eye can see.

OVERLEAF: Near Kom Ombo a heavily laden felucca with billowing sails navigates the waters of the Nile.

LEFT: A typical sight along the shores of the Nile. A group of people have just disembarked from a small ferry onto the sandy banks of the river.

RIGHT: A baby crocodile that has been caught in a fishermen's net. Once extremely common, these animals have almost disappeared from the lower regions of the Nile.

OPPOSITE: Feluccas at the port of Luxor, the site of the ancient city of Thebes. It has become a key tourist destination, with people flocking to see the modern city's ancient splendours, including the temple complex of Karnak. The Valley of the Kings and Valley of the Queens lie across the Nile on the west bank.

BELOW: Two schoolgirls, with veils covering their heads, take a stroll along the river after finishing their studies.

OVERLEAF: The city of Esna stretches out along the left bank of the Nile.

OPPOSITE: A young Egyptian archaeologist involved in conservation work on one of the monuments at Karnak. Along with the temple of Luxor, this archaeological site is one of the most spectacular complexes in the whole of Egypt.

BELOW: The village of El Gourna lies along the Nile and is very popular with tourists. This house, like many others, has been decorated with eye-catching designs, mixing popular motifs with imagery from Ancient Egypt in an attempt to attract passing trade.

OVERLEAF: A peasant steers his boat through the swampy shores of the river, laden with bundles of sedge.

CHAPTER SIX

The Oases of Egypt:
The Other Face of the Nile

PRECEDING PAGES: The old town of Qasr al-Dakhla is the principal settlement in Dakhla, a large oasis composed of a series of small lakes and springs, surrounded by dense vegetation and cultivated plots of land. The centre of Qasr consists of a labyrinth of paths and houses made from crude bricks. New buildings have sprung up over recent decades, and the traditional picture-postcard image of an oasis in the desert has been lost.

OPPOSITE: Irrigation channels at Dakhla. This oasis region is situated in the desert of western Egypt, on the edge of the Great Sand Sea, which stretches from the Nile to the Libyan border.

ABOVE: One of thousands of mummies found in the ground around the Bahariya Oasis. Excavations, which are still in progress, have uncovered so many underground tombs that the area has been renamed the Valley of the Golden Mummies.

ALEXANDER THE GREAT TRAVELLED THROUGH HERE, and after him, Cleopatra. Maybe she was on her way from Thebes, modern-day Luxor, and maybe her beloved Antony was waiting for her at the oasis of Siwa, in the days when he was still rich and powerful. Here we are in a different Egypt. The desert stretches away to the west of the Nile. The Great Sand Sea extends as far as the Libyan border, and it is said that the roots of the Egyptian civilization, which was later to flower along the banks of the Nile, stem from this place. In Neolithic times this area was all savannah. Gazelle were hunted, and lions roamed.

Today, the sand has covered over a primordial civilization, which has slowly slipped away into oblivion over the centuries, systematically eradicated under layers of sand. There are only a few relics of antiquity to be found in this area, mainly around the oases. At Kharga, not far from the course of the Nile, there is the solitary temple of Hibis, which dates from the sixth century BC. A little further away, on the summit of a hill, the Coptic Christian necropolis of al-Bagawat rises up out of the desert, a complex of tombs made out of mud bricks dating from sometime between the fourth and sixth centuries AD.

The oases of Dakhla are an abundant source of water, with at least 520 different springs. One after the other, they stretch for dozens of kilometres, with the crest of a pink-ochre coloured mountain forming a wonderful backdrop, which blocks off the horizon like a piece of theatre scenery. Verdant green paddy-fields glisten in the sunshine, defiant in the face of the sand besieging them on all sides. Herds of oxen are grazing, and flocks of white egrets are circling overhead. Groups of date palms whisper together like scheming guards – sentinels posted along the edge of the desert.

The village of Bashindi seems to be straight out of the pharaonic era: all the walls are smooth and polished, with curved surfaces and winding stairways. Doors and windows tend to be oval or round.

Pastel colours predominate, as if carefully selected to avoid any clash of colour with the desert, which encroaches menacingly at the north gateway to the village. The mountain of sand is kept at bay by intertwined palm branches, but it is an uphill struggle. The mausoleum of Pasha Hindi rises out of the sand. The cupola is Islamic in style, but the structure underneath dates from Roman times. Dotted around it are eight surviving Roman tombs. The sarcophagi have been despoiled over the centuries and lie open, gaping at the blue sky, like useless stone vessels. The nearby palm grove at Qasr al-Dakhla looks like a picture postcard, nestling on the slopes of Mount Sioh. The houses are four or five stories high, and are made out of dark mud bricks. The doorposts have engraved beams, and some of the architraves bear pharaonic inscriptions. Goodness only knows where they came from originally.

We are back in the desert again, between yellow sand dunes. Some of the ones we have just passed are formed from fossil sediments. Perhaps they were once part of an ancient riverbed formed by a branch of the Nile. There are no archaeological ruins at the oasis of Farafra, only simple habitations whose walls have been adorned with multicoloured designs. Most of them represent the haj, the pilgrimage to Mecca undertaken by the families who live there. Some of them are naive pictures of ships and aeroplanes; others depict falcons, birds, gazelle or horses.

'Unfortunately people are now watching television instead of dedicating themselves to traditional arts and crafts,' exclaims Badr, his eyes blazing with indignation. He is the Bedouin artist who has been chosen as the official artist-in-residence in Farafra. His house is a museum of polished stones, of rocks with anthropomorphic forms, and contorted roots resembling claws. He executed the wall fresco using a stick on wet mud. Before it dried, he drew an entire scene composed of different faces: austere profiles, common people, shepherds, peasants; homeless fellahin transformed into epic characters by his hand. Thanks to these faces the artist has become famous. His works have been displayed in Europe and in Cairo, and for once he has been plucked from oblivion amidst the desert sands.

Still more desert lies ahead, but this time it is white, achingly white – a geological miracle manifested in pillars of calcium carbonate, snow-white pinnacles and chalky monoliths that resemble lonely giants. They are all formed from limestone. We reach the dilapidated oasis of Bahariya, where a series of underground tombs have been discovered containing around 10,000 coffins. This treasure trove for archaeologists has been renamed the Valley of the Golden Mummies. Maybe it will become the new Luxor.

A tower formed from limestone in the White Desert, one of the natural wonders of the desert in western Egypt, which spreads north from the Farafra Oasis. Some of these rock formations resemble human figures or giant busts. Others look like the silhouettes of animals: elephants, gazelle or lions. There is little infrastructure: most trips involve off-road vehicles, camping on the sand and sleeping in a tent, although the desert safari's unimaginable wonders make up for its discomforts.

LEFT: In the heat of the evening at the Farafra Oasis, a group of men play a type of draughts on the sand, using small stones. Many of the 5,000 inhabitants have Libyan blood in their veins, or more precisely Senussi blood from Cyrenaica. The women do not have to wear a veil and look strangers straight in the eye, without fear of meeting their gaze.

RIGHT: Summer harvest time near Dakhla. Thanks to the supply of water, the oases are very fertile which enables the cultivation of cereal crops, rice and vegetables. This oasis stretches for dozens of kilometres along the crest of a pink-ochre mountain ridge, which looks like a theatrical backdrop on the horizon. The green fields glisten in the sun, a defiant splash of colour against the encroaching sands that surround them. Herds of oxen graze, flocks of white egrets circle in the sky, and groups of date palms whisper together like scheming custodians.

In the courtyard of one of the houses in Qasr al-Dakhla, dough is being prepared. Before baking, the loaves are left to rise on wooden platters.

OVERLEAF: At the Farafra Oasis there are no archaeological ruins, but simple dwellings adorned with various painted designs. Most of them depict the haj, the pilgrimage to Mecca undertaken by the occupants of the house. Some of the designs are naive illustrations of boats and aeroplanes; others come from local traditions and depict falcons, birds, gazelle and horses.

LEFT: Bashindi, part of the Dakhla Oasis. The mud houses have been moulded by thousands of hands rounding the corners of the walls, and thousands of feet wearing away the steps. Colourfully dressed women frequent the narrow streets.

OPPOSITE: Two old fellahin sitting outside, enjoying the refreshing evening breeze that blows in from the desert.

FOLLOWING PAGES: Beyond the oases, the desert stretches into infinity – thousands of kilometres of dunes and not a single drop of water. Going west, the first well is at al-Khofra, but by then you are already in Libya. The desert here is known as the Great Sand Sea. According to legend, the fearless army led by the Persian king Cambyses II tried to conquer the whole of Egypt in 525 BC, but got lost here, in this vast expanse of nothingness.

LEFT: An old woman plaiting a cord of vegetable fibres near the Farafra Oasis.

RIGHT: A young girl on her way to fetch water from a well at the Farafra Oasis.

OVERLEAF: North-west of Farafra, near the springs of Ain Della, the desert assumes peculiar and fantastical shapes, as if an unknown hand had sculpted the sand. It is possible to imagine a large lake here, stretching to the mountains in the background; ten thousand years ago, when the area was still savannah, perhaps there would have been giraffe, antelope and lions. In other areas, the white of the desert is flat and endless, the surface ruffled here and there like the waves of the sea gently breaking on the foreshore.

'Hermits? Yes, they still exist,' says Father Macario, a Coptic monk. 'They are monks who are in contact with God. But we do not know which of our brothers belong to this order – they will not tell us.' He has black eyes and dark skin, and strokes his long beard, which reaches down to his belt. 'You Catholics – you don't know a great deal about mysticism. Yet you should remember that it was an Egyptian, Saint Anthony, who founded Christian monasticism, and who lived here in this desert, which extends to the east of the Nile, for many years, after overcoming the devil.'

Saint Anthony of Egypt was born into a wealthy family in AD 251, in the city of Alexandria, and abandoned a life of luxury to follow the Gospel. At first he travelled across the desert with the anchorites, in search of a life apart, in search of 'anachoresis'. The Egyptians were amongst the first people to follow the teachings of the Gospel. During the first few centuries after Christ, the patriarch of Alexandria was as important as that of Rome or Constantinople, and claimed to be a direct descendant of Saint Mark the Evangelist. The schism happened in 451 with the Council of Calcedonia, when the Egyptian Christians, the Copts, were ex-communicated following accusations of Monophysism, a tenet of belief that Christ was only divine, not human.

However, the division did not seem to damage the popular faith of the Egyptians. Coptic tradition held that when they were fleeing Palestine, the Holy Family escaped from the persecution of King Herod by following the course of the Nile from north to south, finally arriving at Asyut. Every year on 24 June, there is a festival marking the arrival of the Christ Child in Egypt. Grottoes and gorges, which are traditionally places the Holy Family took refuge, become places of worship. Over the course of many centuries, many monasteries and churches sprung up on the banks of the Nile, which have miraculously escaped the advent of Islam.

Two Coptic monks at the monastery of Saint Anthony, tucked away in the desert of western Egypt. While the Catholic world has become more and more secularized, in Egypt there has been an increase in the number of believers. Over the last few years there has been a religious revival, which has shaken up the Coptic community, composed of around ten million Christians. There are a dozen or so monasteries in the desert that have been affected by the revival. Looking at the map, it is possible to trace a kind of pilgrimage, from the upper reaches of the Nile, across the desert, finally arriving in Alexandria, the seat of the Coptic papacy.

LEFT: At the monastery of Saint Paul, the first mass of the day is celebrated at five o'clock in the morning. The service lasts for several hours, and then the monks set about their daily tasks: cooking, tending the vegetable garden or studying. This is the moment of the Eucharist.

RIGHT: Some children in the subterranean grotto of the Deir al-Adhra church where, according to popular belief, the Holy Family took refuge during the flight into Egypt. The current religious revival is mainly a monastic renaissance amongst the wealthy classes: it is the sons from rich families who are choosing to pursue a monastic life within the confines of the order. Old churches are being renovated and new ones built. Until a few years ago, there were only a few hundred monks; now there are around 2,000. Thousands of pilgrims are flocking to monasteries all over Egypt, particularly during religious festivals.

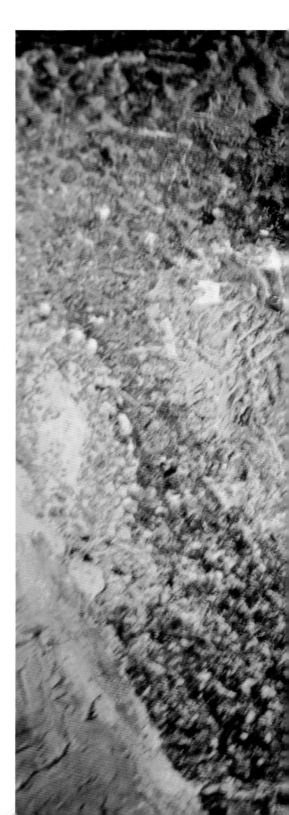

LEFT: The bearded face of an Orthodox Coptic monk from the monastery of Deir al-Baramus, situated in a desert depression called Wadi Natrun, not far from the road that runs between Cairo and Alexandria. In this region there are four Coptic monasteries quite close together, the only ones still in existence out of an original fifty that were built during the first centuries of Christianity, when those who believed in the Gospel took refuge in the desert, in order to escape persecution firstly from the Romans, and then from the Muslims.

OPPOSITE: In the church of Deir al-Adhra, a woman caresses an image of the Holy Family on the flight into Egypt. This episode is particularly important to the Copts as it took place in their native land.

OVERLEAF: A moment during Morning Prayer at the monastery of Saint Paul.

OPPOSITE: Shoes are removed as a sign of respect before entering the church for mass.

RIGHT: A Coptic priest from the monastery of Saint Anthony prepares to bless the bread, which will then be distributed to worshippers during the celebration of the Eucharist.

LEFT: Sophisticated designs in the interior of al-Muallaqah, 'the hanging church', in Coptic Cairo, the oldest part of the Egyptian capital. Cairo is situated on what was a strategic point on the Nile, on the site of the fortified Roman city of Babylon. Since those days, the course of the river has altered by half a kilometre or so. Coptic Cairo is undergoing intensive restoration work to recapture its former splendour.

OPPOSITE: Common stylistic designs found in religious buildings in Egypt, both Christian and Muslim. These are from various mosques in medieval Cairo.

OVERLEAF: The walls of the Deir al-Suryan Monastery at Wadi Natrun, which have become rounded through centuries of wear and tear.

PAGES 228–29: A view of the Nile from Gebel el-Teir.

CHAPTER SEVEN

In Search of the Mediterranean

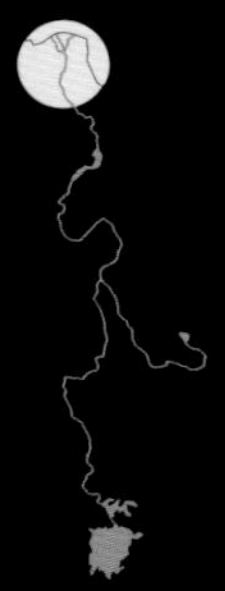

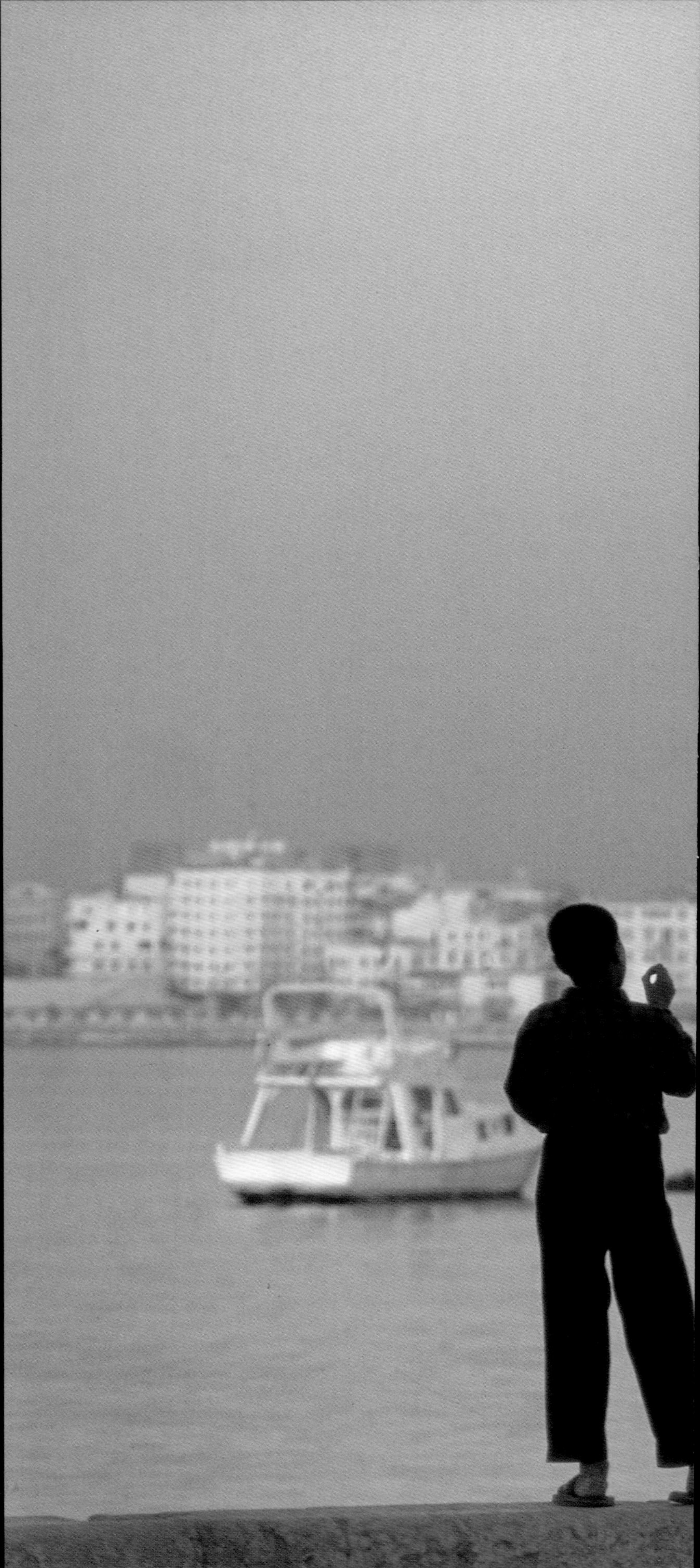

BY THE TIME THE NILE ENTERS CAIRO, it is exhausted, slow and solemn. It looks as wide as the sea, as sprawling as the city against whose foundations it laps. Cairo is an enormous city, with around fifteen million inhabitants – a fifth of the population of Egypt. It is a magma that engulfs and consumes everything in its path, animate and inanimate – a vast, ever-growing and unpredictable volcano. Cement is its lava flow, in the form of huge buildings, strips of road, viaducts and junctions. The pyramids are being swallowed up by the city suburbs. The Sphinx, guardian of the desert for centuries, now gazes out on an urban jungle. It cannot be a pleasant view for the great pharaohs, Khufu (Cheops), Khafre (Chephren) and Menkaure (Mycerinus). Even the Nile, the source of water, has been overwhelmed by the city, engulfed by the eruptions of the metropolis that has robbed it of its splendour and relegated its banks to the passage of traffic. They have become curves of asphalt, where the screeching of threadbare tyres on cars and lorries competes with squeals of brakes, the sound of skidding and horns blaring.

There is no harmony between man and water here – they are mutually antagonistic. The ancient heart of the city was known as Babylon, and was situated at a strategic point on the Nile, the cradle of the earliest Christianity. These days this area is known as Coptic Cairo. The Nile has shifted by 400 metres since those times. Nowadays that ancient heart has become an oasis of peace, contrasting with the hive of activity and the hubbub of noise in the rest of the city. The city has turned its back on the great river of the tenth century, when the rulers of the Fatimid dynasty built their new Islamic city not far from its banks. Since that time, Cairo has grown relentlessly, century after century. Today, the ancient Islamic district is incredible. It is boisterous and chaotic, a tangle of streets, cafés, markets, shops, donkeys, children, vendors, carts, mosques, Islamic schools and minarets. Dark and derelict ruins are flanked by sumptuous buildings, reflecting the glory of the sultans who lived in times of greater prosperity than now. Squalor and splendour lie side by side.

Despite the restoration work that is in progress, Cairo looks the same as it did in medieval times. It never ceases to amaze visitors. That thought is echoed by Naguib Mahfouz, the Egyptian winner of the Nobel prize for literature: 'Wherever you look, your eyes come to rest upon an engraved doorpost, an ornate window frame, the elegant silhouette of a minaret; or perhaps your ears pick up the strains of an ancient incantation coming from the gatehouse of a takiya, chanted by a mysterious dervish. The people who live here come from all walks of life: there are workers, craftsmen, amulet-makers, quacks, layabouts, scoundrels, employees, wheeler dealers, and people selling all kinds of things.'

The lava from this crater flows for miles, encompassing the old and the new, the Citadel of Saladin, modern Cairo, the Nasser area, the new suburbs and the city of the dead – a sad cemetery inhabited by immigrants who have sought shelter among the tombstones. This erupting volcano changes its topography every day. It is impossible not to get disorientated in a city like this, and not just geographically. History and memory are intertwined and layered one upon the other, to such a point that dates and references become confused. Secular life stratifies and settles into layers of sediment, in the same way as the emotions and the amazement invoked by this impossible synthesis. What a city! Such a place could only have been created by the great river.

When the Nile senses that the Mediterranean is near, it widens out of all proportion at the delta, and laps against the city of Alexandria. It does not inundate the city, but skims lightly around it. There is no other river in the world that links two such cities. A three-hour drive from Cairo, Alexandria is the second biggest megalopolis in Egypt, and on the Nile. Over four million people live here. The street named the Corniche begins at Montaza, the port on the delta, and stretches along the coast for twenty or so kilometres, penetrating the heart of the city. Following this street, we encounter Ptolemaic Alexandria. The Ptolemaic dynasty (c. 332–30 BC) was founded by Ptolemy I, a general under the command of Alexander the Great, and marked a fusion of Egyptian and Greek cultures. In those days it was a city of supremacy: its lighthouse was one of the Seven Wonders of the Ancient World, and its library became the largest in living memory. Later on, in Roman times, it became the city of Cleopatra. Then it became the Vatican of the Copts, after the split with Rome. At the beginning of the tenth century, it was the Paris of the Mediterranean, a cosmopolitan city that hosted Greeks, Lebanese, Italians, Maltese, Maghrebians and Jews. Another Nobel Prize winner, the Italian poet Giuseppe Ungaretti, who was born in Alexandria, put it like this: 'This city, which is my own city, wears you down and destroys you incessantly.' It was like that in those days, and it is like that still.

The sprawling periphery of Cairo now almost reaches the three famous pyramids and the Sphinx at Giza. The photograph shows a corner of the pyramid built by the Pharaoh Menkaure (Mycerinus).

OVERLEAF: Cairo is a city that never sleeps, even at night. The photograph shows a branch of the Nile flowing around the island of Zamalek, considered to be one of the most chic districts of the Egyptian capital.

LEFT: Mirrors in the popular Café Fishawi at Khan al-Khalili, the entrance to the medieval quarter in Cairo. This is one of the most fascinating parts of the city – densely populated, with a large number of monuments, mosques and noble old residences.

OPPOSITE: A young man, carrying freshly baked traditional loaves, weaves his way along the winding streets of Khan al-Khalili.

OPPOSITE: Cairo's cafés have traditionally been the preserve of men, but now they are being frequented by women. Cairo is one of the most open capital cities of the Arab world.

RIGHT: Tea is an essential part of the café culture in Cairo.

The Islamic quarter in Cairo is a maze of alleyways, with an infinite number of shops and workshops representing a thousand different activities. Below, a shopkeeper sells items made from aluminium and tin. There is always a hustle and bustle of people, carts, peddlers, stalls and donkeys. The air is thick with different aromas. It is a cross-section of life in Cairo, a life that has often provided the backdrop for the literary works of the Egyptian Nobel prize-winner Naguib Mahfouz.

OVERLEAF: The recently restored mosque of Sabil Kuttab Shayk Mutahharil. For years the area has been a building site. The authorities in Cairo want to restore the most important monuments in the history of the medieval city to their original splendour. There are at least a hundred and fifty of them, including mosques, minarets, madrasahs, mausoleums, inns and merchants' houses, with carved wooden doorways and windows with gratings so that women could watch the world go by without being seen.

The most important buildings in this area are the Al-Azhar University and the citadel, a spectacular medieval fortress that was once the residence of the sovereigns of Egypt.

LEFT: A view of the covered market at Qasaba Radwab-bay in the southern district of medieval Cairo, not far from the Bab Zuweila gateway, one of the poorest areas of the city.

OPPOSITE: The decorated doors of the Salib al Wafa'iyya mosque.

OVERLEAF: The spectacular marble tiling that adorns the interior of the madrasah of Sultan al-Nasir Hasan, an impressive religious building built in the fourteenth century. On the left of the photograph is the mihrab, the niche that faces Mecca, and on the right is the minbar, the pulpit from which the Imam addresses the congregation during prayer.

LEFT: The immense chandeliers suspended from the cupola of the equally immense mosque of Muhammad Ali, constructed in the first half of the eighth century and situated within the walls of the citadel.

OPPOSITE: A detail of plaster tracery work found in the mausoleum complex of the Mameluke Sultan Qalawun. The complex dates from the thirteenth century, and consisted of a madrasah and a hospital in addition to the mausoleum.

LEFT: The Muslim cemetery, referred to as the 'city of the dead'. The largest tombs have been taken over by homeless people, often peasants who have come here from the countryside. Even some of the mausoleums of the Sultans and Mameluke princes have been converted into dwellings. The photograph shows the necropolis running along the outer side of a wall, which was constructed in the period of the Fatimid caliphs of medieval Cairo, beyond the Bab al-Nasr gateway.

RIGHT: The custom of smoking a shisha, or water pipe, is widespread among men in Egypt, who congregate in the many bars in Cairo's medieval quarter. The pipes take at least half an hour to smoke, and the tobacco is strongly perfumed.

The myth of Alexandria was shattered, disintegrated, but has now been reborn. The Pharos lighthouse, which had been swallowed up by the sea over the course of several centuries, was given new life in the fifteenth century by the Arab conquistadors, who used its foundations in the construction of the Qayt Bay Fort, a Mediterranean outpost. Moreover, a new and amazing library has risen from the ashes of mythology. The ancient Library of Alexandria, believed to have been the world's first major seat of learning, housed works by such masters as Socrates and Plato but was destroyed by fire many hundreds of years ago. The new library, made out of granite stone from Aswan, looks like a UFO watching the sea and shines down on the city. A symbol of Babel, its circular walls are inscribed with all the different alphabets known to man, past and present. It's an impressive building, boasting eight million books, three museums, five research institutes, one planetarium and a conference hall, which can hold up to 3,000 people.

Saad Zaghloul Square looks out over the Mediterranean Sea. Young people are kissing on the Corniche, despite the girls' veils. Secessionist palaces surround us, and a sense of liberty. Wrought iron work: gates with swirls and flowers, elegant grilles with Arabic script, competing with the cacophonous arabesques of an imposing villa that belonged to an Egyptian magnate in a wealthier epoch. These links to the past are more reminiscent of Paris and Rome than Cairo – breaths of wind from the heart of Europe, crystallized in architecture that is now shabby and dilapidated. A few horse-drawn carts are returning from the Attarine district. There are four crossroads, and then the orthogonal roads give way to a labyrinth of small streets full of boutiques and workshops. A variety of merchandise is on offer: chairs and sofas, fruit and vegetables, eggs and narghile, bicycle wheels and waste pipes, children and old people all absorbed in selling something or doing something. Life rushes on relentlessly, never ceasing.

At sunset, a travelling vendor wanders around in search of business in Saad Zaghloul Square, the bustling centre of Alexandria. In the background, the vast harbour is just visible, providing a safe haven for fishing vessels and recreational boats.

OVERLEAF: The futuristic silhouette of Alexandria's new library. Looking like a flying saucer that has fallen from the sky, it faces out to the Mediterranean Sea.

LEFT: A 'wall of books' opposite the new library. Completed in 2003 with the help of international donations, it has set itself up as a centre of culture in the heart of the Mediterranean, like the famous ancient library built in the third century BC during the reign of Ptolemy II. In its heyday, the library was said to have held between 40,000 and 700,000 books. This epic centre of classical culture was destroyed by a fire, the cause of which is still a subject of controversy amongst scholars.

OPPOSITE: One of the library's circular walls, made out of granite from Aswan, which has been inscribed with all the past and present alphabets of the world – a symbol of the Tower of Babel and the confounding of knowledge. The library receives 800,000 visitors each year and has become a point of contact between Islamic and Western cultures. In addition to holding eight million books, many of them extremely valuable, the library also has three museums, five research institutes, a planetarium and a conference hall with 3,000 seats.

OPPOSITE: The façade of the Greek café Pastroudis. Along with many other restaurants and establishments run by different nationalities, it symbolizes the multi-ethnic nature of the population during the golden days of Alexandria, when the city was regarded as the Paris of the Mediterranean.

RIGHT: The sun sets behind the silhouettes of the cupolas and minaret of the Abu al-Abbas Mursi mosque, a notable example of twentieth-century Islamic architecture. It is situated not far from the banks of the eastern harbour.

OVERLEAF: The Qayt Bay Fort, constructed in medieval times to defend access to the eastern harbour of the city. This imposing structure was built on the site of the legendary lighthouse of Alexandria, the Pharos, one of the Seven Wonders of the Ancient World. Built in c. 280 BC, it stood 150 metres high. Chunks of the original lighthouse were found during archaeological investigations that explored the waters surrounding the fort.

Craftsmen busy in the artisan district of Attarine, an area also famous for its second-hand and antique shops – the most genuine in town. Here most of life is lived outside, on the street. This shop seems to be selling a bit of everything, from eggs to old paintings.

OVERLEAF: A game of volleyball on a floating platform, which has been tethered in the bay by the yacht club.

OPPOSITE: In Attarine, the collecting of old newspapers and paper is a constant activity, as it is a source of money. In Alexandria, history is everywhere, although it is true that memories of the Hellenistic period have all but disappeared. The city was founded by Alexander the Great and intended to be the capital of an empire. Its architecture was imposing, and it became a destination for scholars and experts during the reign of the Ptolemies, who came to power after the death of Alexander. There are far more relics from the Roman domination, such as the amphitheatre and the temple of Serapis.

BELOW: A group of carpenters pose in their workshop in Attarine. Like Cairo, Alexandria has many immigrants: country folk who have come to the city in search of work, bringing their traditions with them. The opulent palaces of the nineteenth century are a reminder that, for a short period, before the construction of the Suez Canal, the city experienced the brief hope of once again becoming 'the pearl of the Mediterranean'.

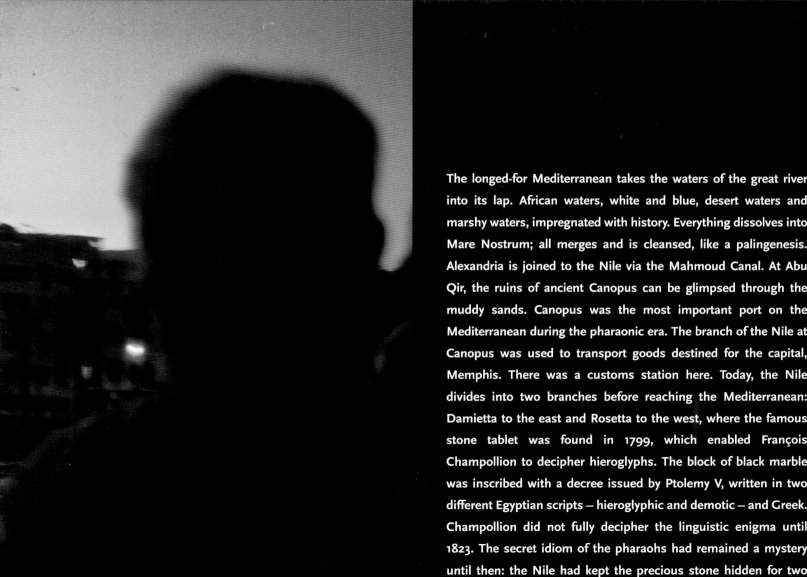

The longed-for Mediterranean takes the waters of the great river into its lap. African waters, white and blue, desert waters and marshy waters, impregnated with history. Everything dissolves into Mare Nostrum; all merges and is cleansed, like a palingenesis. Alexandria is joined to the Nile via the Mahmoud Canal. At Abu Qir, the ruins of ancient Canopus can be glimpsed through the muddy sands. Canopus was the most important port on the Mediterranean during the pharaonic era. The branch of the Nile at Canopus was used to transport goods destined for the capital, Memphis. There was a customs station here. Today, the Nile divides into two branches before reaching the Mediterranean: Damietta to the east and Rosetta to the west, where the famous stone tablet was found in 1799, which enabled François Champollion to decipher hieroglyphs. The block of black marble was inscribed with a decree issued by Ptolemy V, written in two different Egyptian scripts – hieroglyphic and demotic – and Greek. Champollion did not fully decipher the linguistic enigma until 1823. The secret idiom of the pharaohs had remained a mystery until then: the Nile had kept the precious stone hidden for two

PAGE 1: Bas-relief from the tomb of Ramesses VI, Valley of the Kings, Luxor.

PAGES 2–3: The magnificent Murchison Falls.

PAGES 6–7: Sunset over Queen Elizabeth National Park, Uganda.

PAGES 8–9: Pyramids at Meroë, Sudan.

PAGES 10–11: The palm groves along the Nile at Esna, Luxor, Egypt.

Translated from the Italian *Nilo: Dal cuore dell'Africa alle rive del Mediterraneo* by Clare Costa

First published in the United Kingdom in 2006 by Thames & Hudson Ltd, 181A High Holborn, London WC1V 7QX

www.thamesandhudson.com

Photographs © 2006 Aldo Pavan
Original edition © 2006 Magnus Edizioni SpA, Udine, Italy
This edition © 2006 Thames & Hudson Ltd, London

British Library Cataloguing-in-Publication Data
A catalogue record for this book is available from the British Library

ISBN-13: 978-0-500-51325-5
ISBN-10: 0-500-51325-2